W9-BKA-992

ANIME

ESSENTIALS

ALSO BY GILLES POITRAS

The Anime Companion:
What's Japanese
in Japanese Animation?

ANIME

ESSENTIALS

EVERY THING A FAN
NEEDS TO KNOW

Gilles
Poitras

Stone Bridge Press
Berkeley, California

This book is dedicated to all the anime fans who have stayed up nights

discussing the significance of the Macross Valkyrie transformation . . .

• •

PUBLISHED BY

Stone Bridge Press, P.O, Box 8208, Berkeley, CA 94707

TEL 510-524-8732 • sbp@stonebridge.com • www.stonebridge.com

The publisher would like to extend its thanks to all the studios, artists, and companies that cooperated in the publication of this book and the acquisition of images. Your help and generosity are greatly appreciated! We have done our best to contact rightsholders and to faithfully and accurately credit all copyrighted materials. Please advise us of any oversights and omissions.

10 9 8 7 6 5 4 3 2 1   2005 2004 2003 2002 2001

Anime Essentials: Every Thing a Fan Needs to Know
by Gilles Poitras
ISBN 1-880656-53-1

CONTENTS

AND NO DANCING TEAPOTS!

Welcome, whether you are an anime beginner (the person I wrote this book for), a curious parent wondering what your children have gotten into, or a fan firmly entrenched in the pleasures of viewing anime. I hope this book will be enjoyable and useful for you. For those new to anime fandom, welcome to an established fan culture unlike any other. A world where speech is peppered with Japanese terms, where SM refers to a little girl's show, where children's entertainment is as intelligent as that of adults, and where the values of sincerity, courage, and perseverance are very important.

If you ask the average American about Japanese animation—forget esoteric terms like "anime" much less genre-specific terms like "shōjo anime"— and they will think of *Speed Racer, Astro Boy, Robotech, Pokémon,* or other edited and rewritten shows broadcast on TV. These shows are all fine and good in their own way, but the diversity, quality, and quantity of anime is so great that the subject deserves a closer look, especially through releases that have been neither edited nor rewritten, where the original creator's intent is better preserved in the translation.

What is anime?

Anime (pronounced ah-nee-may), as defined by common non-Japanese fan usage, is any animation made in Japan. In Japan, the word simply means "animation." While anime is sometimes erroneously referred to as a "genre," it is in reality an art form that *includes* all the genres found in cinema or literature, from heroic epics and romances to science fiction and comedy.

Why watch anime? Because it is enjoyable. Do you really need a better reason? But anime has a lot more to offer than pure entertainment. An entire subculture has grown up around anime and its related entertainments, not only in Japan but worldwide, although there has been almost no recognition of this by the U.S. press.

Outside of Japan, anime has become *the* major way in which non-Japanese are exposed to Japanese culture. Unlike Japanese cinema, anime has rapidly spread via video releases to a growing audience. While you have to hunt for stores renting and selling Japanese cinema, anime is much easier to find. One reason for this is that the range of available anime is much more diverse than that of imported Japanese cinema, so it can attract a wider range of ages.

Anime is primarily produced for children and young adults. But so much of it is so sophisticated when compared with the American product that adults often become fans of shows intended for a much younger audience. I have discovered that if you show non-Japanese adults an anime title and ask them to guess the intended audience age, they will often overestimate the target age by ten years or more.

I must tell you that this book is necessarily limited in scope. There are plenty of anime titles available in English, but they represent only a small percentage of the thousands of titles that have been produced to date in Japan. This book is not even a complete overview of all the English-language titles—anime is too vast and complex to do that in one volume. It is, instead, an orientation designed to get you started enjoying anime or to help you enjoy anime more.

Of course, as with everything that a person "discovers," there is an urge to share the discovery with others. So when you get hooked on anime, try not to be too annoying to your friends and acquaintances (but a little annoying is OK).

Titles used

The English titles in this book are generally those that are commonly used in the U.S. These are not always literal or even accurate translations of the original Japanese titles. Sometimes the titles for subtitled and redubbed editions of the same anime are different: *Fushigi Yūgi* and *Mysterious Play* are the same series, but the first is subtitled and the second redubbed. Anime released in the Commonwealth countries (Britain, Australia, etc.) may yet have different titles.

Not all of the works mentioned in this book are available in English; in some cases it may be several years before anyone picks them up for English-language distribution. For anime not yet available in English I give both the title in transliterated Japanese and the common English title. Not that any of this guarantees consistency; for example, the title currently known as *Night Warriors* was at one time commonly known as *Vampire Hunters* and as *Darkstalkers*.

• •
Otaku = fan

You will often hear anime fans referred to as "otaku." There's some interesting history here. The Japanese word, written as a combination of the Chinese character for "house" and the honorific prefix o-, can be translated as "your honorable house." It is an exceedingly polite way of saying "you" when addressing another person in conversation. For many of the shy and socially inept young males who are anime and manga fans in Japan, such a distancing and formal way of speaking to others became a common affectation. The writer Akio Nakamori proposed in a column that the term be applied to the fans themselves. The usage stuck, and "otaku" is now used by the media to describe anyone who is highly obsessed with a particular subject, not just anime. These days fans all over the world are calling themselves otaku with pride. But there are also discussions (I mean arguments) among non-Japanese on Usenet newsgroups over the *exact* meaning of the term, since the Japanese media sometimes use it to denote extreme—and dangerous—fixation.

About *Otaku no Video*

Throughout this book I include images from the 1992 anime mockumentary *Otaku no Video*. This anime depicts the activities of some very hardcore fans (otaku) in Japan, and I single it out for special attention in this book because it provides such a wonderful (and at times disturbing) portrait of anime fans who are totally into their obsession. I must thank K. J. Karvonen who told me how *Otaku no Video* could be seen as a training manual for otaku if one simply made a point of studying the activities of the protagonists in the story. Thus the anime serves much the same purpose as this book.

If you rent or buy this title—and you should—you will note how the characters refer to their "science fiction club" activities. In Japan anime fandom is often organized into science fiction clubs, since SF is a major anime genre and one of the main starting points for budding otaku. *Otaku no Video* occupies a special place in my heart as its characters seem so darn familiar to me. I have known many people involved in the U.S. science fiction fan scene for years, and there is something about such serious fans that just translates across cultures.

Here is a challenge for people who think they are serious anime fans. Watch *Otaku no Video.* Is your experience different from what's shown in the film? Have you done all that crazy stuff? Make a list of whatever you have not done—yet. Next, list all the hidden and not-so-hidden anime references you can find in *Otaku no Video.* Then read the liner notes AnimEigo, the U.S. distributor, provides to see what you've missed. Now, watch a lot more anime to fill in those gaps, and consider adding some of those activities to your own anime experience.

ABOUT THE COVER

While we're on the subject, I should point out that the cover of this book is taken from *Otaku no Video.* The image contains a number of visual references to anime and to Gainax, the company that made *Otaku no Video.* The central figure, Misty May, is a reference to the main character of the animation done for the opening ceremonies at Daicon IV, a major science fiction convention held in 1983. Bunnies, either animal or girls in suits, are a cute motif in some anime. The little girl to the left is a reference to the "magical girl" genre of anime. She transforms into Misty May with the help of her wand (just think

OTAKU NO VIDEO My own copy of the tape is autographed by Mr. Yamaga of Gainax Studios. This is the same image used on the cover of this book.

of the transformations in *Sailor Moon*). At the top of the image we see Tanaka (sitting) and Kubo (standing). Tanaka is based on Toshio Okada and Kubo on Hiroyuki Yamaga, two of the founders of Gainax. To the best of my knowledge, the young woman to the right does not depict a real person, although one never knows for sure with *Otaku no Video.* The lion cub is modeled after another lion cub, King from *Nadia,* another famous Gainax work.

One final note

As this work is intended for the U.S. and Canadian anime fan, it does not cover many aspects of anime culture in other parts of the world. In fact, anime has huge followings in England, Europe, Australia, and throughout Asia, including Korea and Taiwan. Titles released into those markets may differ from those presented here, and of course every country has its own particular fan culture and available activities, such as conventions. Nevertheless, much of the material in this book will apply regardless of the country it's being read in, since many of the examples I mention throughout this book are designed to be representative of anime in general.

AND A FINAL FINAL NOTE
ON NAMES AND WORDS

All names in this book have been Westernized; that is, they are presented with the personal name first, followed by family name: thus, Hayao Miyazaki, not Miyazaki Hayao. This is the reverse of how names are given in Japan. For historical reasons, Japanese names are the only ones Americans do this to; we don't, for example, reverse Chinese, Korean, or Vietnamese names. Scholarly works do not do this name flipping, and perhaps popular works will eventually follow suit. But I bow to popular pressure so as not to create confusion, since most U.S. distributors and anime magazines continue to release material from Japan with the name order reversed. So don't blame me. (However, this situation may be changing. Some U.S. distributors have been using Japanese name order for a while now, and the same practice is now also seen on the English pages of the web sites of some Japanese companies.)

I've generally followed standard methods of romanizing Japanese words (a "long sign" as in $\bar{o}$ and $\bar{u}$ indicates an extended vowel sound, for example). Because studios and artists sometimes adopt nonstandard spellings for their names, characters, and works when presented in English text, wherever possible I've tried to honor those preferences. Most often, it is the long sign that is omitted.

Acknowledgments

There are several people who deserve special recognition for the assistance they gave me in the writing of this book.

Helen McCarthy, who wrote the first English-language book on anime, *Anime! A Beginner's Guide to Japanese Animation* in 1993 and encouraged me to write this book.

Steven Farnum, long-time fellow anime viewer, whose many comments and questions regarding anime over the years have in various ways influenced parts of this book.

Trulee Lee, a past president of Cal-Animage Alpha, whose anime and manga recommendations since the days when she was a student have been helpful, even if occasionally of dubious taste <grin>.

The folks at Mikado-Laser Japan in San Francisco's Japantown, who helped me obtain Japanese DVD discs of *Otaku no Video* and the *You're Under Arrest* OVAs so I could do image captures without the subtitles.

Peter Goodman, my publisher and editor, because he had to cope with my delays and lots of the details that would have pushed me further over the edge. Thanks Peter, to you and the gang at Stone Bridge Press, for helping me get this book done.

And of course all the companies, Japanese and American, who generously granted permissions to use images from their products in this book.

Some individual staff members of these companies stand out for their particular helpfulness:

Robert Woodhead, Natsumi Ueki, and Shin Kurokawa of AnimEigo, who all assisted in various ways by answering my questions and giving me bits of advice.

Harumitsu (Harry) Miyazaki of Toshiba EMI. His quick reply to my request to use *Otaku no Video* images in this book broke all speed records.

Hiroyuki Yamaga and Hiroki Sato of Gainax for helping me obtain permissions from one of my favorite companies.

Nobu Yamamoto of Bandai Entertainment, who while buried alive in work was still able to assist me.

Gamal Hennessy of Central Park Media, who was able to get me images from most of the titles I requested.

Thanks, everyone!

Gilles Poitras
Oakland, California

HOW ANIME IS RELEASED

Assuming you will be watching a lot of anime from now on, it would be good to ask, How the heck did all this stuff get here? Historically, anime has been released in three ways.

Theatrical release

Until the 1960s and the spread of television, animation was released worldwide only in theaters, first as short works shown with regular films and later as features in their own right.

Today, theatrical-release anime movies can be stand-alone, brand-new features or related to earlier series. When tied to an earlier series, a movie can be a side story, a condensation or retelling, or even a final episode to a TV series, as was the case with the first *Kimagure Orange Road* movie in 1988.

Theatrical features are also often later rereleased on Laser Disk (LD), DVD, and VHS tape.

Terebi (television)

Television grew increasingly popular in Japan in the late 1950s; by 1960, over 29 percent of homes had a set, so it was only a short matter of time before anime made for TV began to appear. A classic show, Osamu Tezuka's *Tetsuwan Atom* (1963), also known by its English title, *Astro Boy*, was among the earliest televised anime series.

TV is still a major distribution medium for anime. In the monthly magazine *Animerica* Takashi Oshiguchi notes that during the fall season of 1998 there were around twenty *new* weekly anime shows on TV. Not all were for regular broadcast, as mountainous Japan has an extensive satellite broadcast system. But even so, imagine being a fan and trying to keep up with all the new shows.

Many television shows are later rereleased on Laser Disk, DVD, and VHS tape.

ASTRO BOY Many non-Japanese still think this long-familiar, lovable character is representative of all anime. Boy things have changed!

OVA/OAV

With the development of video players for the home, a new market appeared for anime. These titles produced for direct sale to rental shops and collectors are known as OVAs (Original Video Animation, also referred to as OAV).

Some anime that are considered too financially risky for theater or TV release will still be profitable if sold as OVAs. Candidates for OVA release may be in a special genre with a limited audience or may have content—drugs, violence, sex—inappropriate for Japanese TV.

One advantage of the OVA format is that it allows ideas for a series to be tried out with less risk; if successful, a TV series may result. A classic example of this is *Mobile Police Pat-*

labor, which started as an OVA series in 1988, became a TV show, and then became a second OVA series and several movies.

If an OVA series does not sell well in Japan, it may simply end mid-story, as was the case with the well-made *Mighty Space Miners* (1995) and some other series.

Video formats

The ways anime is sold on video are:

VIDEO TAPE
Standard video cassettes are a very common media for anime distribution. Japan uses the same VHS NTSC format found in the United States, and this has aided the spread of anime to North America.

LD: LASER DISC
Long a popular medium among very serious anime fans, Laser Disc has better-quality images than VHS. Many anime titles have been easier to get from Japan on LD than on tape, since Laser Disc technology is more common in Japan than in much of the Western world. Recently the Japanese LD market has been steadily eroded by a growing DVD market.

VCD: VIDEO COMPACT DISC

The Video CD is a minor format not well known in the U.S. It is being rapidly replaced by DVD. Video CD has been more popular in Hong Kong and Taiwan and has a reputation for being widely used by the bootleg video market.

DVD: DIGITAL VERSATILE DISC OR DIGITAL VIDEO DISC

Rapidly becoming a major medium for video, DVD has the great advantage of carrying multiple sound and subtitle tracks so that a single disk can have dialogue in more than one language as well as subtitling in several languages. Some companies are adding extras such as remote-controlled, menu-driven image or text files. Imagine a reference book on the same disk as the film, or even a spoken commentary on a separate audio track, similar to what has been done with DVD releases of some classic movies.

A major limitation for some anime fans is the region coding of the DVD format instituted by manufacturers to help solve their licensing, piracy, and export problems. A DVD disc can thus be set to play only on players configured for certain geographical zones. It is possible to lock a disc to one region or to several regions or to make it regionless. This means that buying a disc made for Region 2, which includes Japan, is not an option for fans with conventional U.S. players, which are Region 1. When you sort through anime DVDs in a store or at a convention, be sure you select those that match the region of your player. Further information can be found in your DVD player manual and on the packaging of the DVD itself. Here are the region codes currently in use.

> Region 1: United States, U.S. territories, Canada

> Region 2: Europe, Japan, the Middle East, Egypt, South Africa, Greenland

> Region 3: Taiwan, South Korea, Philippines, Indonesia, Hong Kong

> Region 4: Mexico, South America, Central America, Australia, New Zealand, Pacific Islands, the Caribbean

> Region 5: the former Soviet Union, eastern Europe, India, most of Africa, North Korea, Mongolia

> Region 6: China

ERAS OF ANIME

1917–62:
the early, pre-TV era

The earliest examples of commercial animation produced in Japan, starting around 1917, were fairy tales, of both Japanese and Western origin. These early films used the same animation techniques found elsewhere in the world at that time, such as single images with backgrounds (a very labor-intensive process), cut-out images laid on top of background images, and, in time, cels (see-through overlays that include multiple foreground and background images).

A note on target and viewing audiences

The target audience for anime is not exactly the same as the actual viewing audience, as many adults will watch shows aimed at children while kids will watch anime intended for older audiences. One feature of the history of anime is how the age of target audiences has gone up over the years. Anime has grown older at a slower rate than its viewers, but over the past decades it has gradually moved from targeting small children exclusively to providing sophisticated titles for adult viewers as well.

During Japan's fascistic period before and during World War II, artists were heavily censored and often restricted to producing propaganda or were not allowed to work at all. One interesting militaristic piece of work from this era is the theatrical feature *Momotarō no Umiwashi* (1943), which included a fleet of ships manned by cute animals engaged in naval battles with the Americans, in particular the attack on Pearl Harbor. This obviously propagandistic piece of work was funded by the Ministry of the Navy. Strapped by content restrictions, the animators nevertheless managed to make improvements in animation techniques that would prove useful in the future.

The decade after the war was a hard one for both anime and cinema due to the great damage inflicted upon the country. Many theaters and production venues had been destroyed. All the same, the manga industry grew as a cheap form of entertainment that did not require buildings and projectors; one could easily rent manga from special shops, predecessors to video stores. As the 1950s progressed, the Japanese movie industry recovered and began to flourish; directors like Kurosawa and Ozu became world famous. Anime was not left behind, as funds and resources for animation work became easier to obtain and new movie theaters were opened.

•••••••••••••••••••••••••
Manga

Manga is the term used for Japanese "comic books." Manga is not a synonym for anime, tho' some older folks and nonfans sometimes use it as such. Fans of anime in Japan don't particularly care to have anime called manga, much as English-speaking fans of fine animation object to it being called "cartoons." Even in anime you occasionally hear nonfans refer to anime as manga; two examples are the drunk in *Otaku no Video* talking to the heroes while they wait one night for an anime movie to premiere and Yukina in *Martian Successor Nadesico* showing a lack of appreciation for her older brother's love of the *Gekiganger 3* anime. Manga can include almost every subject imagin-

LESSONS FROM OTAKU NO VIDEO #1

©1991 GAINAX / YOUMEX

A cel being painted by Kubo. When an animation cel is painted, the details are done first, and then the larger areas are painted in. Painting on the back of the cell lets the front be smooth when photographed. Painting the details first also enables you to quickly apply paint to the larger areas. But be careful to stay within the lines! Should you stray, let the paint dry and then scrape it off carefully. In the credits of some of your anime you will find the name of the person who mixed the paints.

able, from gag comedy to serious literature; technical manuals and even legal case histories have been released in manga format. For more on manga, see Fred Schodt's *Manga! Manga!* and *Dreamland Japan*, two excellent books on the topic.

The 60s: the birth of modern anime

In 1962, Mushi Productions, a studio founded by the famous manga artist Osamu Tezuka, released its first animated theatrical title, *Aru Machikado*

17

no Monogatari (*The Story of a Certain Street Corner*). Meanwhile, the development and spread of television was creating a new potential market for anime. In June 1962 the first animated TV show, the Otagi company's *Manga Calendar,* aired; the program continued until August 1964.

• •

Osamu Tezuka (1928–89)

One of the most influential writers in postwar Japan, occasionally referred to as the "god of manga," Osamu Tezuka produced a huge amount of manga and animation. In his manga he pioneered many innovations in style and form that are common to this day. A fan of cinema, he incorporated many of the stylistic forms of film into his work, giving the impression that the drawings could have been stills from movie sequences. He also pioneered many of the manga and anime genres that were to have a major influence on later artists, including erotic, girls', and ladies' manga.

The ground had been broken. In 1963, Mushi Productions began showing its first TV anime, *Tetsuwan Atom*; NBC was soon broadcasting the program in the United States, redubbed into English and retitled *Astro Boy.* The program was based on Tezuka's 1950s

LESSONS FROM OTAKU NO VIDEO #2

©1991 GAINAX / YOUMEX

While our heroes eagerly wait in line late at night for the next day's premiere of *Nausicaä of the Valley of the Wind,* they have to put up with the incomprehension of an intoxicated passerby. This guy just doesn't get it. Not only does he not understand why anyone would wait for a premiere showing of an anime, but he gets ticked off when he is addressed in a very formal manner. Luckily the woman with him is a lot nicer and gets him to move along.

manga *Atom Taishi* (Ambassador Atom) and had been preceded by a live-action show in 1959. This one title effectively represents the beginning of the linkage between manga, live-action shows, and anime, a close connection that is responsible for much of the financial success of Japan's modern publishing and entertainment industries.

In *Tetsuwan Atom* we see a thematic motif that turns up again and again in Japan: the doll with a soul. In the West we have the Pinocchio story, but in Japan there is the added element, from an old folk belief, that a doll loved and cared for could develop an actual soul. From *Tetsuwan Atom* to *Saber Marionette* (1995), the fuzzy borders between the mechanical and human come up again and again. There is an added twist in *Ghost in the Shell* (1995), where the cyborg Major Kusanagi expresses doubt over her humanity after almost all of her original body has been replaced by machinery.

GHOST IN THE SHELL The interpreter for a government official seems like everyone else until you look below the surface.

The theme of cybernetic humans in anime also goes back to the fruitful year of 1963 with the *8 Man* series about a murdered detective whose mind is transferred to a mechanical body. This show enjoyed a following in the U.S. on TV in the mid-1960s, decades before the *Robocop* movies.

The year 1963 was also when the first anime program that could be described as a giant robot show aired: *Tetsujin 28-Go* (*Iron Man 28*). Unlike *Astro Boy*, here the machinery is not human sized and autonomous but huge and radio controlled.

In time the giant robot subgenre evolved to where the robot's control came from a pilot working inside it; this would prove a popular mechanism in a wide variety of stories in later years. These programs all presented technol-ogy not as inherently frightening or dangerous but as a force for good or evil depending on who got the power and control. This could be described as an appropriate view for a society that had seen dictatorial political and military power ruin an entire nation as well as its neighbors, but had then witnessed it reborn thanks, in part, to technological advances directed by a democratically elected government.

Tetsujin 28-go

Starting in 1966, part of the *Tetsujin 28-Go* series was shown in an edited form on U.S. TV as *Gigantor*. Over the years I have been surprised at the number of people who are not anime fans but who remember this title with great fondness. Now if only that same nostalgia hook could get them to watch more anime!

The 70s: the junior high through college years

As the young viewers of the 1960s anime shows grew older, the studios started to produce programs for a slightly more mature audience. In the 1970s the giant robot idea of *Tetsujin 28-Go* inspired a flood of programs, no longer in black and white but in bright colors. These robots were not limited to anthropomorphic, or even animal, shapes but could transform into other machines or even segment into several parts; each part had a pilot who could recombine the units into the major giant robot of the story as the episode approached its climactic battle.

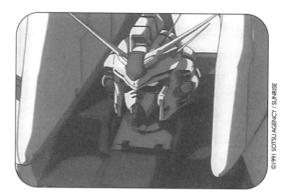

GUNDAM 0083 A close-up of the head of a Gundam unit showing similarities with a *kabuto*, a traditional Japanese warrior helmet.

© 1991 SOTSU AGENCY / SUNRISE

• •
The U.S. invasion

The 1980s saw many of the shows from the 1970s released on U.S. TV. *Gaiking, UFO Robot Grandizer, Getter Robot G,* and *Dangard Ace,* along with the hero show *Starzinger,* were cut to twenty-six episodes each and packaged as a group of programs under the collective name *Force Five.* Go Nagai's popular *Manzinger Z* was shown as *Tranzor Z* in 1985 (why they changed the name I don't know). Marvel Comics even licensed several of the designs and used them, under other names, in their *Shogun Warriors* comic book series.

A major feature of the giant robot stories—and of many similar live-action shows—is the team, which usually includes an older scientist, a few young men (one of whom is the pilot), a young woman, a kid, and occasionally an animal mascot. Also of note are the robots' head designs, many of which greatly resemble the ornate helmets or *kabuto* worn by high-ranking samurai warriors during Japan's feudal years when the land was wracked by war among rival fiefs. The horns, crescents, and other ornaments of the *kabuto* are not the only aspects of these shows influenced by Japan's rich tradition of martial arts; hand-to-hand combat is also crucial to the giant robot shows, which often feature close-quarter axe, sword, and spear combat between large hunks of mechanized metal.

Great heroes and epic stories became prominent in the 1970s with the television and theatrical releases of several anime based on the dramatic works of the masterful manga writer Leiji Matsumoto. The most significant of these anime were *Uchū Senkan Yamato* (*Space Battleship Yamato*, 1974–75), *Uchū Kaizoku Captain Harlock* (*Space Pirate Captain Harlock*, 1978–79), and *Ginga Tetsudō 999* (*Galaxy Express 999*, 1979). Matsumoto even did a giant robot manga, *Wakusei Robo Dangard A* (*Planetary Robo Dangard Ace*), which was animated in 1977–78. Matsumoto's tales of heroism, of courage, and of humanity and suffering set against the backdrop of the vast panorama of space and strange worlds continue to captivate viewers.

Harlock and the queen

Through abundant splicing and rewriting, two unrelated Matsumoto-based anime done by different studios—*Uchū Kaizoku Captain Harlock* and *Shin Taketori Monogatari Sen-Nen Joō* (*The New Taketori Story: The Queen of a Thousand Years*)—were combined into a single English-language TV series in 1985 under the title *Captain Harlock and The Queen of a Thousand Years.*

Several Leiji Matsumoto anime and manga placed on a poster advertising the release of the *Queen Emeraldas* OVA.

My own exposure to anime came in 1977. I was in San Francisco's Japantown and saw a TV in a shop window with *Uchū Senkan Yamato* playing on it. I could not understand the language, but I was a fan of cinema, and the use of pacing and "camera" angles as well as the science fiction theme quickly caught my attention. The visual structuring of the action struck me; it was very different from any American animation I had ever seen, and much more like European cinema.

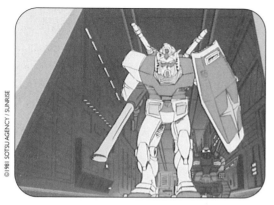

MOBILE SUIT GUNDAM: THE MOVIES The Gundam Unit launches into battle.

● ●
Yamato blazers

Uchū Senkan Yamato was shown on U.S. TV in 1979–80 as *Star Blazers*.

In 1979 there appeared a giant robot show that mixed humanism with a cold dash of realism. The original *Mobile Suit Gundam* series was the creation of Yoshiyuki Tomino, and for over twenty years now the Bandai studio has been producing a series of profitable Gundam TV shows, movies, and OVAs, with little sign of stopping. Tomino even wrote a novelization of the original *Gundam* series (with some departures from the original storyline) that was translated into English by Frederik L. Schodt and published in the U.S. in 1990 as *Gundam Mobile Suit*.

But the 1970s was not only a time of science fiction adventure. It was also a period that saw an expansion of the genres being made into anime. A prime example is the numerous *Lupin III* anime that began coming out in the 1970s based on the manga of an author with the unlikely nom de plume Monkey Punch. *Lupin III* is a humor- and action-laden pastiche of the 19th-century French super-thief character Lupin, James Bond, American gangster films, and samurai adventurers of Japan's Edo period (1600–1868).

The 80s: anime matures

The 1980s saw further development of anime storylines as well as a significant expansion in genre, improvements in technique, and the flowering of major new talents bringing their works to audiences.

In 1981 came the first animated version of *Urusei Yatsura*, based on the manga work of Rumiko Takahashi, a young woman whose writings would grow to delight millions worldwide. *Urusei Yatsura*, the story of a young high school lecher who ends up "married" to an alien princess, added new elements of absurd humor and fantastic situations, and it produced the first anime pin-up girl, Princess Lum. *Uru-*

sei Yatsura would run on TV for several years and spawn a series of OVAs and movies. The U.S. company AnimEigo started releasing *Urusei Yatsura* on subtitled video in 1992; the TV series alone will be represented by about fifty VHS tapes or DVD discs with four episodes per tape or disc by the time the series is fully released.

In 1982 came *Chōjikū Yōsai Macross (Superdimensional Fortress Macross)*, a show with music playing a major role in the plot and the young singer Lynn Minmay as an important *chara*.

Chara

Chara is simply a shortened Japanese way of saying "character." Fans have adopted this usage not so much in speech as in Usenet newsgroups and in Internet chat groups, where any way of saying something with fewer letters is welcome.

In 1983 *Crusher Joe,* based on the space-opera science fiction novels of Haruka Takachiho, was released into theaters. *Crusher Joe* contained a movie within a movie (featuring a drive-in theater and the first appearance of Kei and Yuri from *Dirty Pair*, another series from Takachiho's works). *Dirty Pair* also went into animation and was

to prove even more successful as OVAs, a TV show, movies, and even a second OVA series—with a younger Kei and Yuri—called *Dirty Pair Flash*. After all, who can turn down a show about two independent, strong, attractive young women who always create a lot of collateral damage, even when it's not their fault?

Mari Iijima

Mari Iijima, the actress who was hired as the voice of Minmay, did some acting on U.S. TV following that role. She now lives in California and concentrates on her singing and songwriting career, which had been her focus before she began acting. In 1999, much to the delight of fans, she began touring the North American anime convention circuit to promote her albums. While most fans were more interested in her acting role in *Macross*, many discovered, or rediscovered, her singing and bought her albums. To date she has over fifteen albums out.

December 1983 saw the release of the first OVA, *Dallos*, directed by the talented Mamoru Oshii, who was a significant figure in the making of many of the *Urusei Yatsura* anime and whose career continued to rise. Later he would solidly establish his reputation with works such as *Mobile Police Patlabor*, *Angel's Egg (Tenshi no Tamago)*, *Ghost in the Shell, Jin-Roh,* and even live-action movies like *Jigoku no Banken.*

In 1984 the direct-to-consumer nature of the OVA led to a new development in anime: the sexually explicit erotic story, a genre that had long existed in manga. The first erotic OVA was a two-story set featuring *Yuki no Kōge-shō* (*Reddening Snow*) and *Shōjo Bara-kei* (*Girls Tortured with Roses*). This was quickly followed by the first OVA in the famous *Cream Lemon* series.

In March 1984 the important work *Nausicaä of the Valley of the Wind* (*Kaze no Tani no Nausicaä*), written and directed by Hayao Miyazaki, was released in the theaters. *Nausicaä* established Miyazaki's reputation as a masterful director and is considered by many to be one of the best anime ever made. The title character was so popular with fans that for the rest of the century she was always in the top twenty of female anime characters in *Animage* magazine's annual poll.

In 1987 came the release of a title that was to elevate the standards of storytelling and animation. *The Wings of Honneamise,* also known as *The Royal Space Force*, was the story of a young man's maturation from a passive member of an obscure government organization to a dedicated astronaut. But it was more than that: it featured a whole and complex society with its own customs, styles of clothing, and architecture. Many fans were astonished to learn that the anime was the very first professional production of what was then a new company called Gainax. Gainax has continued to extend the reach of animated storytelling ever since.

Akira, written and directed by Katsuhiro Otomo and released in 1988, proved a major eye-opener for many non-Japanese when it was shown in art house theaters in the English-speaking world in 1991. The combination of an unchildlike style and spectacular animation was like nothing a U.S. audience had seen before. *Akira*'s impact was so huge that for the entire decade it was probably the single anime most familiar to adult non-fans in America since the 1960s.

THE WINGS OF HONNEAMISE Some members of the Royal Space Force are seen off as they board a ship on their way to the launch site.

The end of the decade was signaled in 1989 with the death of Osamu Tezuka, who had done so much to shape and transform anime and manga. His work over several decades had established both media as valid forms of artistic expression as well as powerful entertainment.

Several significant anime series spanned the last years of the 1980s and ran well into the 1990s.

Starting in 1989, Rumiko Takahashi's *Ranma 1/2* manga became the basis of an extended series of TV shows, OVAs, and movies. By the mid-90s, *Ranma 1/2* started appearing in the U.S., the anime and manga released by Viz Communications in San Francisco, a subsidiary of Shōgakukan, the Japanese company that produced the originals.

The studio Headgear started its *Mobile Police Patlabor* (*Kidō Keisatsu Patlabor*) series with several OVAs in 1987–88; this was followed by a TV show in 1989, then movies, and then more OVAs in 1990–92, some of them revisiting stories from the TV show as well as climaxing a major TV subplot. A manga version of the story was also published, drawn and written by Masami Yuki, a founding member of Headgear.

PATLABOR A Patlabor unit takes on the Griffon from one of the most famous story arcs in this popular series.

The 90s: the explosion of diversity, the worldwide spread of anime

The early 1990s saw a rise in both the number of companies producing anime in Japan and the number of companies distributing anime in the rest of

25

the world. Despite the bursting of the bubble economy and the recession that followed, the Japanese anime and manga market did not decline until the very end of the decade. Anime has proven to be an inexpensive form of entertainment that has helped support the industry through Japan's lean years. As viewers matured in taste and age, the market began to demand more complex narrations as well as a higher-quality product. Many titles were produced that could not be watched in a half-attentive manner. Works like *The Hakkenden* (1990–95) and *Perfect Blue* (1998) would seem like beautifully crafted confusion to anyone who did not pay attention to the story. In both of these anime the story goes from straightforward narrative to marked complexity to a resolution more sophisticated than is seen in most live-action films.

The 90s was also the period of several OVA/TV/movie crossover series. The most famous of these was *Tenchi Muyo*. The franchise began in 1992 as a series of OVAs; then came a TV show followed by movies, another TV show, and even a spin-off series—called *Pretty Sammy*—of OVAs and a TV show.

Little girls' (*shōjo*) anime also made

THE VISION OF ESCAFLOWNE Yukari (with the long hair) chews out Hitomi for being late to track practice in the anime's first episode.

a big splash with shows like *Sailor Moon* in 1993. If nothing else, *Sailor Moon* proved that a TV program aimed at the four-to-twelve-year-old age range could not only be a successful way to merchandise products in Asia but could also be profitable in wider international distribution.

● ●
Shōjo

A girl or young woman. The term specifically refers to the age group between the onset of puberty and marriage, usually in the mid- to late twenties. A significant portion of the entertainment industry in Japan aims at this gender specific market, with much of the creative work being done by women.

The market for shōjo anime also expanded greatly with titles such as *Fushigi Yūgi* (also known as *Mysteri-*

26

ous Play, 1995–96) and *Revolutionary Girl Utena* (1997–98). At times, in shows like *The Vision of Escaflowne* (1996), it crossed over into the male market with works that mixed traditional genres. *The Vision of Escaflowne* mixes the character development and concern for feelings of shōjo programs with the action and machinery found in boys' shows. While the U.S. TV release of *The Vision of Escaflowne* cut many of the shōjo scenes and turned the program into more of an action show, the unedited videos are available for those who wish to see what the original show was like.

In the 1990s a highly successful manga-producing team of young women from Osaka known as Clamp had a major impact when several of their titles, such as *Campus Detectives*, *Magical Knight Rayearth*, and *Card Captor Sakura*, were made into children's TV anime. Other anime based on their works include the *X* movie anime and the tongue-in-cheek, all-female bondage and discipline OVA homage to Lewis Carroll called *Miyuki-chan in Wonderland* (1995).

The age range of anime viewers took a great leap forward in Japan in October 1995 with the release of the *Neon Genesis Evangelion* science fiction TV series. This show, with its deft handling of human drama, captivated many adults who, while they openly read manga, would rarely have confessed to watching anime. *Neon Genesis Evangelion* even spun off a lot of merchandise aimed at an adult market, such as digital phones and even laptop computers with the logo of the story's major organization, NERV, on them. This success was not without controversy, since the series had been broadcast early enough in the evening that children could watch it, and a few episodes had controversial content, such as a scene where two unmarried chara are in bed together having a conversation (all off camera, but still pushing accepted content standards a little too much for some folks).

Genderbent Card Captor

In the summer of 2000 a highly edited version of *Card Captor Sakura* was aired on U.S. network television as *Cardcaptors*. Many of the character names, and even the relationships between some characters, were changed. Ads gave the impression that this girls' show was actually a boys' action program.

Another series that reached older audiences with more sophisticated stories was *Cowboy Bebop* (1998), a tale of bounty hunters in the Solar System of the future. *Cowboy Bebop*'s smooth blend of film noir, Hong Kong–style martial arts, cool jazz, and science fiction produced a compelling show that further expanded the barriers of anime. This time broadcasters were more cautious, and some episodes of *Cowboy Bebop* were not shown on regular TV but only via digital satellite broadcast.

Another science fiction TV anime to push the envelope in the late 1990s was the complex and somewhat existential *Serial Experiments Lain.* The show was not only commercially successful but was awarded a prize at the 1998 Media Arts Festival by Japan's Agency for Cultural Affairs.

Anime's fan base had definitely solidified. By 1992 fandom had reached such a level in Japan that Gainax could release *Otaku no Video,* a delightful albeit disturbing mockumentary of fans (otaku) and fan culture. Fans now not only watched anime, but they also produced it and even created titles making self-conscious allusions. *Martian Successor Nadesico,* which aired on TV from November 1996 to April 1997, is a full-fledged science fiction anime series filled with references to fan cul-

COWBOY BEBOP Fay Valentine and Spike Spiegel are two bounty hunters with questionable pasts of their own.

ture and even featuring an old-style giant robot team anime show, *Gekiganger 3,* as a major part of the plot. *Nadesico*'s success resulted in an increase in the video release of older 1970s programs and in the making of new robot shows in a style similar to those of the past but with modern production values.

In the 1990s computers started being used more in Japanese animation, albeit in ways quite different from U.S. productions. Some works, such as

28

Macross Plus, Ghost in the Shell, Princess Mononoke, and *Blue Submarine No. 6,* mixed cel animation with computer-generated images to produce striking effects. Computer-drawn animation also became more common in the late 1990s, with companies shifting to drawing their cels not with paint but with digital-imaging software. Fuji Film even took the step of announcing that it would stop producing cels for the animation industry, leading to a scramble on the part of anime companies to import cels from other countries and transfer more production to digital painting. As the 1990s ended, new styles of computer-generated animation could be glimpsed in video games such as *Final Fantasy VIII.* Fully computer-generated movies are now in the works in Japan, again with a look very different from that of similar films being made in the U.S.

The 1990s also saw the flow to the English-speaking world of commercial, translated anime go from a slow trickle to a flood. More and more Japanese companies either established divisions for the English-speaking market or licensed the rights to other, often new, anime-only companies. These overseas companies not only released anime to video at a higher speed as the decade neared its end, but they even released some titles to video before they were available in Japan and coproduced such titles as *Ghost in the Shell* and the *Tenchi Muyo* movies.

©1998 SATORU OZAWA / BANDAI VISUAL / TOSHIBA EMI / GONZO

BLUE SUBMARINE NO. 6 One of the nonhuman women in this anime reacts in fear when her sisters threaten a man she saved from drowning. This image is almost entirely a cel painting.

©1998 SATORU OZAWA / BANDAI VISUAL / TOSHIBA EMI / GONZO

BLUE SUBMARINE NO. 6 One of the biologically modified whales used to attack human settlements, this creature carries a variety of weapons, including small armored craft and torpedos. This image is almost entirely computer generated.

©1990 TEZUKA PRODUCTIONS

KIMBA THE WHITE LION A young Kimba looks across the plains of Africa. Many fans of this show never knew it was from Japan.

The growth of English-language fandom

The existing anime fan community in the English-speaking world had been growing slowly since the 1970s. But in the 1990s the number of fans dramatically increased. Fans organized into more clubs, started more conventions, and launched several English-language magazines devoted to anime and manga.

Anime fandom in the English-speaking world is sometimes referred to by the term "generations," a way of grouping fans who were introduced to anime by a particular film or program. As I was beginning work on this section, I had done nothing more than produce an outline with notes. Then I saw Bruce Lewis and Cathy Sterling's article "Come Alive! You're in the Anime Generation" in the May 1999 issue of *Manga Max*. I was struck not only by the similarities to my outline (both the authors and I drew from the same fan vocabulary), but by the differences. I refer you to this article for the details.

THE ASTRO BOY GENERATION
In the 1960s there were many Japanese titles on TV, but few fans really got their start from these. Instead this early period exposed viewers to the medium of animation and increased their receptivity toward anime later on.

THE EARLY FANS (AKA THE OLD TIMERS)
Early fans cut their teeth on *Speed Racer, Eighth Man,* and *Battle of the Planets,* a very butchered version of *Kagaku Ninja Tai Gatchaman.* What distinguishes them from many of the viewers of earlier shows like *Astro Boy* and *Kimba the White Lion* is the fact that they discovered that what they liked was a Japanese product and searched for more.

THE YAMATO GENERATION (AKA THE STAR BLAZERS GENERATION)
Star Blazers is the English title of the

Uchū Senkan Yamato series, hence the double name of this fan generation. *Star Blazers* originally aired in 1979–80. One reason this series gained loyal fans is that its single strong narrative required addicted viewers to make sure they made it home in time so as not to miss an episode.

THE ROBOTECH GENERATION

The earlier series did not generate that many fans who recognized anime as a Japanese product with significant differences from American animation. The earliest major generation, at least in the U.S., is perhaps the Robotech Generation, named after the 1985 TV show created by cobbling (some would say butchering) three unrelated shows into one. Fans of *Robotech*, plus those introduced to anime by watching *Star Blazers*, were to form a significant number of organized fans in the 1980s.

THE AKIRA GENERATION

The film *Akira*, which played in art theaters in December 1989, produced a cult following. Some of the viewers moved on to become fans of other anime, but many stalled there and saw *Akira* as an isolated work, thus missing the creative context of anime and manga that it represented. This genera-

MACROSS Two variable fighters. One is in a fully transformed mode and the other is half transformed into the so-called Gerwalk mode. In flight mode, these warrior machines look much like modern jet fighters.

tion, if it is a generation at all, is smaller than the earlier ones simply because not many people could actually get to one of the few theaters that was showing *Akira*.

THE SAILOR MOON GENERATION

In the 1990s something new happened in the U.S. Previous generations of fans were largely of college age; even many of the Robotech Generation hadn't become fans until years after they had seen their first show. Then, in 1995, the anime show *Sailor Moon*—whose heroes are girls—began its run on American TV. *Sailor Moon* caught the attention of large numbers of viewers who were in high school and even grade school, and many of them were girls. In only a few months, fan demo-

LESSONS FROM OTAKU NO VIDEO #3

©1991 GAINAX / YOUMEX

Kubo is frustrated with his job-hunting and has found out he has been dumped by his girl-friend; when he called, a man answered her phone. He wonders aloud as to why anime otaku are looked down on, since no one has ever looked down on his love of tennis. Finally he rips off his tie and proclaims that he will refuse to give in. He will become an otaku of otaku, an otaking! Tanaka likes the idea and rips off his tie, and the two lock arms as they pledge an oath to stand together in their re-solve. Then they lose their balance and fall into the fountain beside them.

graphics shifted dramatically. I remember seeing lots of girls and their mothers at the big West Coast convetion Fanime Con in 1997; they were impossible to miss. These fans quickly moved beyond *Sailor Moon,* and as their interests diversified so did the number of titles released into the market. Would *Fushigi Yūgi, The Vision of Escaflowne,* and *Revolutionary Girl Utena* have done as well before *Sailor Moon* hit the U.S.? I doubt it.

THE OTAKU GENERATION

I got the term "Otaku Generation" from Lewis and Sterling's article, where they use it to describe the present generation of fans. I don't know whether this term really applies or whether we will even be able to speak of generations of anime fans in the same sense again. In the past, the release of a title on TV or in the theaters was unusual enough that fans could remember their first anime experience as something very special. But now, with more and more anime on video and with mainstream media critics reviewing theatrical releases like *Perfect Blue* and *Princess Mononoke,* we seem to be entering an era when new fans join the existing community more as a stream than as waves of new converts.

Pokémon has caused quite a stir, but its viewers are so one-show focused that they cannot really be called new anime fans; rather, they are fans of a program that happens to be anime, and it remains to be seen where their interest will take them. *Gundam Wing* and *Card Captor Saku-ra*—two shows currently on U.S. TV—may give us another wave of new fans, as they appeal heavily to junior high and high school students, but this could be the last of such discernible

©2000 GAINAX / PRODUCTION I.G

FLCL One of the tamer scenes in Gainax's odd and humorous *FLCL* (pronounced Furi Kuri). After seeing just a little of this OVA series I want more. Just wait until you see the use of really spicy curry in a fight against a monster at the school.

waves. It is possible that television, especially cable, will be adding enough anime to the broadcast schedules to keep fans moving from one show to the next, sweeping new ones in as older ones graduate to other, more sophisticated shows.

The growing number of serious fans, compared to the number of casual anime viewers, is now becoming a significant factor in marketing decisions by the U.S. distributors. After all, not that many years ago a few video store chains were the predominant market for anime tapes, usually of the redubbed variety and released at the meager rate of one or so per month. Today the fans are such a force that companies are doing things like switching all their subtitled anime to

DVD and packaging lengthy series as whole box sets.

In any case, the combined numbers of all the generations of anime fans now make it easy for us to welcome new fans into our existing networks and help them get access to many titles they probably are not at all aware of. Perhaps Kubo's dream of the otakuization of the world is a little closer.

● ●
Please note

I must confess to not having seen the anime shows that were reshown on U.S. TV in the 1980s as I did not own a TV for over twenty-five years, from the early 1970s until the mid 1990s. I finally bought a TV and VCR to watch anime and then discovered Japanese-language TV on UHF. To write some of the sidebars in this section I had to rely on an article by Ghislain Barbe titled "Heroic Robots of the 70's" in *Protoculture Addicts* numbers 40 and 41 and on the excellent chapter "Animated Television Series Made in Japan and Broadcast in America" from Ledoux and Ranney's *Complete Anime Guide*. Anyone seriously interested in this topic should read these works. See chapter 10 for publication details.

THREE

ANIME GENRES

Genre in anime is a tricky subject. Japanese and American animation genres don't exactly parallel one another; nor are the expressions of genre in Japan quite like those found elsewhere in the world.

For example, *Gundam 0080* (1989) can be described as a giant robot anime. But such a description does not do justice to the story's many layers of complexity dealing with family problems, civilians caught up in war, and friendship between a child and soldier, not to mention the sheer tragedy of death and destruction brought on by war. *Gundam 0080* is no more just a giant robot anime than *War and Peace* is just a war novel.

My advice here is that you not let genres have much influence on what you watch, since the genre itself may not be a good predictor of what the anime is really about: a story of high school romance may appeal to a lover of fine literature, or a lighthearted kid's show may make a fan of gloomy and dark narratives laugh with delight.

Science fiction: the roots of modern anime

Science fiction is the major genre of anime, and this is especially true of the anime titles released overseas. From *Tetsuwan Atom* (*Astro Boy*) of the early 1960s to the present day, science fiction has long played a role in the history of anime. This is partly because anime in the early years was boy-oriented and boys love science fiction, but it is also because one can do interesting science fiction shows in animation without a huge special effects budget. In the past few decades, while the U.S. has been spending tens of millions on a few excellent films with special effects, including computer-generated characters that look like plastic action toys, Japan has been using older cel techniques and putting

©1989 SOTSU AGENCY / SUNRISE

GUNDAM 0080 Al and Bernie have a serious conversation as their mission turns grim.

MECHA AS A ROBOT CULTURE PHENOMENON

A major subgenre of SF involves *mecha* stories. These feature "mechanical" devices that are often, but not always, giant robots. Originally such robots were radio controlled, but in the 1970s anime introduced pilots riding inside the machines, adding a new, human dimension to the drama.

Mecha

The word mecha simply means "mechanical," i.e. "machinery." Anything from an electric shaver or steam train to a huge anthropomorphic fighting machine with a pilot inside, or externally controlled by a young boy, is mecha.

out many more well-crafted and entertaining stories at a fraction of the cost.

Science fiction is so popular in Japan that SF clubs are found in schools, even at the college and university level. One might ask, why? Is it due to a love of technology? To the fact that school clubs are highly encouraged by educators? Or is it just that there is so much material available—in anime, manga, and live-action shows, as well as tons of foreign imports—that just about anyone will feel at home there? In *Otaku no Video* (1992) there is an interview that mentions the many non–science fiction attractions of such a students' club, including mah-jongg games and girls' school uniforms. (But then anything said in *Otaku no Video* must be treated with a certain degree of skepticism, tho' I believe the part about the girls' school uniforms. . . .)

Perhaps the ultimate mecha series is *Mobile Suit Gundam*, which since 1979 has been made into several TV series, movies, and OVAs. A central theme of *Gundam* is that of civilians caught up in war doing the best they can in difficult or deadly situations. The magnificent *Mobile Suit Gundam 0083* OVA series (1991–92) is perhaps one of the best examples of this. A young civilian engineer tries to carry out her job servicing the equipment her company designs for the military while, at the same time, coping with the emotions of being in a war zone and seeing people she knows killed or imperiled. This stark tale of determination is complicated by factions in both militaries vying for power and influence, even when it means the death of their own soldiers.

RACE IN SCIENCE FICTION ANIME

Many science fiction anime feature characters of different races or who themselves are racially mixed. After all, in a space story taking place in the future, not everyone can be Japanese. For example, most of the chara in *Macross Plus* (1994–95), set on the colony world of Eden, are of mixed ancestry. Even stories set in Tokyo have chara who are not Japanese, or are of mixed ancestry, such as Nene Romanova in the *Blade Runner*–inspired *Bubblegum Crisis* OVA series from the late 1980s.

GUNDAM 0083 Nina Purpleton, as she sees a friend on Earth.

©1991 SOTSU AGENCY / SUNRISE

OTHER SF GENRES
AND SCIENCE FANTASY

Within the larger science fiction genre are all sorts of subgenres, from vigilante teams (*Bubblegum Crisis*, 1987–91), special agents (*Dirty Pair*, 1985–), and war-story adventures (*GunBuster*, 1988–89*)* to remakes of classic live-action shows (*Giant Robo,* 1993–95), bounty hunters on the frontier (*Cowboy Bebop*, 1998), and massive political epics on a grand scale (*Legend of the Galactic Heroes*, or *Ginga Eiyū Densetsu,* 1988–95).

There is one branch of science fiction so fantastical that it borders on the realm of magic. The works of Leiji Matsumoto are like this: strong, allegorical, almost mythic tales and broad, sweeping adventures whose conclusions take on an almost cosmic significance. Visible in Matsumoto works, especially in the *Galaxy Express 999* stories (animated in 1979 and 1981), is the influence of the writer Kenji Miyazawa (1896–1933), whose transcendent fiction partook equally of Buddhism, technology, and European philosophy.

Another popular example of this subgenre are the several *Tenchi Muyo* anime series of the 1990s that feature powers of flight, moving through walls, time travel, malignant beings with vast powers, and even ghosts.

The manga of Kia Asamiya have also been a source for science fantasy anime, such as *Silent Moebius* (movies, 1991, 1992; TV show, 1998) and the *Compiler* OVAs (1994–95). *Silent Moebius* is the tale of an all-woman team using both high-tech gadgetry and magic to fight against a demonic invasion. *Compiler* is about two women who have come to Earth pursued by others from another dimension. The women have the ability to take on different powers by plugging units into their necks. . . . The whole thing is very entertaining and often quite silly. A recent project is *Corrector Yui* (1999), an NHK anime about people inside a computer world (appropriately, the Asamiya company is called Studio Tron).

Fantasy

The fantasy realm in anime relies either on home-grown material or on myths and fables imported from overseas, and sometimes the resulting products represent a combination of both.

NHK

The Japan Broadcasting Corporation, Nippon Hōsō Kyōkai, is commonly called NHK. This publicly owned radio and TV broadcaster has been operating since 1926. Many significant anime have appeared on NHK.

FANTASY BASED ON ASIAN TRADITIONS

Japan's own folk and religious traditions are a fruitful ground for harvesting ideas for anime. Perhaps the series with the greatest reliance on native traditions is *Blue Seed* (1995), which includes many references to famous locations as well as to Shinto and Buddhist legends and practices. Ninja stories often have a strong supernatural element, and this can be seen in anime and live-action movies like *Ninja Scroll* (1993) and *Curse of the Undead: Yoma* (1988–89), where the main chara and their opponents have superhuman abilities. Rumiko Takahashi, one of Japan's best-known story writers, has drawn heavily on Japanese traditions in her *Urusei Yatsura, Ranma 1/2, Inu-Yasha,* and *Mermaid* manga; but she always adds her own, usually amusing, embellishments. There is also the popular *Vampire Princess Miyu* OVA series (1988–89), which later spun off a TV show.

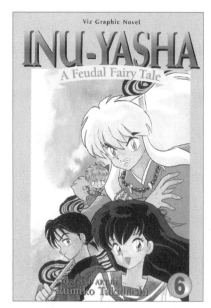

INU-YASHA The cover of a volume in the publisher Viz's release of this manga in graphic novel format.

VAMPIRE PRINCESS MIYU The Japanese box art for *Kyūketsuki Miyu*. The word "Princess" was added by Animeigo when the title was released in the United States.

Shinto

Shinto is the indigenous religion of Japan. The word is written with two Chinese characters that mean *kami* ("divine spirit") and "way," or "the way of the *kami*." Shinto cannot always be spoken of as a single religion; it is instead a body of often local traditions that grew out of a complex history, including the addition of many influences from surrounding cultures.

Studio Ghibli, home of Hayao Miyazaki and his fellow artists, has produced some excellent works set in a Japanese context. These include *Heisei Tanuki Gassen Ponpoko* (1994) with its shape-shifting *tanuki* protagonists fighting to protect their home mountains from a massive construction project in the 1960s; *My Neighbor Totoro* (1988) with its rural spirits befriending two young girls; and the hugely successful *Princess Mononoke* (1997) with its forest gods.

Fushigi Yūgi (1995–96) is an example of a shōjo anime set in a non-Western context outside Japan. The main Japanese characters, two girls, are in a world very similar to ancient China and must bring together two groups of heroes in order to gain the power to have their wishes granted.

Tanuki

A mammal, the tanuki resembles the raccoon in its facial features and build but not much else. In folk traditions the tanuki is considered to have supernatural powers including the ability to change shape and cast illusions. Hefty ceramic statues of male tanuki displaying large testicles, wearing a straw hat, and holding a gourd bottle of sake are sometimes displayed outside shops as decorations.

FANTASY INFLUENCED BY WESTERN TRADITIONS

Western-influenced supernatural and fantasy anime is a more recent genre in Japan, partly due to the relatively late discovery by the Japanese of fantasy role-playing games such as *Dungeons and Dragons*. Perhaps the most famous of the D&D–influenced manga and anime are the *Lodoss War* stories such as the *Record of Lodoss War* OVAs (1990–91) and *Legend of Chrystania* (1995). The *Record of Lodoss War* OVA series was reportedly based on the notes of an actual game played by the authors.

The longest-running series of the Western Sword and Sorcery genre is *Slayers* (1995–). *Slayers* lasted several seasons on TV and also ended up in movies and OVAs. Its tongue-in-cheek style and fast pacing have made it a

RECORD OF LODOSS WAR Highly fanciful pseudo-Western armors and weapons abound in the *Lodoss War* stories.

popular film among many non-Japanese fans.

Hayao Miyazaki's Studio Ghibli has also produced some excellent works with both magic and a Western flavor. *Kiki's Delivery Service* (1989) is about a girl witch and takes place in a mythical town on a seacoast in Europe. *Porco Rosso* (1992) is set along the Adriatic Sea during the pre–WWII Fascist era in Italy and stars a young aviator whose internal torments have

©1995 HAJIME KANZAKA / R. ARAIZUMI /TV TOKYO / SOFTX / MARUBENI

SLAYERS More humorous and less serious looking than the characters in the *Lodoss War* series, the stars of *Slayers* provide action and laughs.

caused his body to take on noticeably porcine features.

Western goddesses have even come to Japan. In the *Oh My Goddess!* OVAs (1993–), Scandinavian goddesses move to modern Tokyo, and Yggdrasil—which in the older tradition was a sacred tree—is now a celestial super-computer requiring maintenance (involving a very interesting and lively debugging process).

Horror

One of the most interesting examples of Japanese horror anime is *Doomed Megalopolis* (1991–92) with its villain seeking vengeance on an entire city. It has sexual content but nothing explicit. Much more direct is the *Urotsukidoji* (1993, 1995) series; one of the first Japanese anime released in the United Kingdom in 1993, its predatory sexuality and disillusioned view of interpersonal relations shocked the British tabloid press. The negative reaction to *Urotsukidoji* ended up victimizing other anime that followed; lazy reporters on both sides of the Atlantic continued to parrot older, hysterical news reports rather than do original research or view the many other films available that were neither gloomy nor unsuitable for children.

©1993 KOUSUKE FUJISHIMA / KODANSHA /TBS / KSS FILMS

OH MY GODDESS! Belldandy is shown enjoying the sunshine and befriending local birds

40

Comedy

Humor has been a part of animation since the early days; after all, you can do some pretty funny things with drawings that are just not possible with live-action films (or were not possible until the recent advent of computer graphics imaging). And many anime in other genres either have comedic moments in them or are full-fledged comedies that transcend the conventional barriers between genres.

Some of the humor in anime is simply slapstick or situational, and much of this translates quite well. The hilarious Sword and Sorcery parody *Dragon Half* (1993) pokes fun at the Role Playing Game clichés of dragons, warriors, and wizards, not to mention women in iron breastplates and skimpy outfits. The added mix of male idol singer, adoring female fans, fast-paced action, and some off-color humor draws laughs from many fans who would not normally watch fantasy anime. When I was once trying to decide what to show next at an anime potluck, someone said, "No big eyes," and I knew I just had to toss in *Dragon Half* with its cute, large-eyed characters.

Some humor does not translate well. With puns and other verbal humor this is to be expected; translators try to substitute other jokes, explain the puns in liner notes, or just ignore them. With some shows the humor is so culturally based that it requires an insider's knowledge. *Ping Pong Club* (1998) is an extreme example of this. It is dense with references to TV shows, theater, and literature. One friend of mine refuses to watch the show, since he knows there is a lot going on but gets frustrated at not knowing what it is. The satire *Otaku no Video* also has

PING PONG CLUB Four of the members of a junior high school Ping Pong club you don't want to get near. Especially the guy in the upper left, or is it lower left or on the right? Oh well, avoid them all.

© 1986 SŌEISHINSHA / FINAL-NISHIJIMA

PROJECT A-KO Typical high school girls with large mecha, super strength, and voices that make grown men cringe.

many anime, manga, and live-action show references.

Crime

Crime and police stories in anime often overlap many other genres. One of the most famous humorous crime shows is the long-running series of TV shows and movies in the *Lupin III* superthief stories that started in the early 1970s. Lupin is a thief who, with his sidekicks Goemon and Jigen, commits several crimes while pursued by the long-suffering and highly determined inspector Zenigata.

• •
Lupin III

Lupin III is an homage to the original character from the turn-of-the-century stories by Maurice LeBlanc. Goemon is a reference to a legendary Japanese thief who is the subject of several Kabuki plays. Zenigata comes from the Edo-period stories about a Japanese crime-stopper.

a high level of referential humor, but it is so woven into an amusing story that fans don't mind not catching all the anime references; in fact, many fans come back to *Otaku no Video* again and again as their knowledge of anime grows, giving them the pleasure of catching what once sailed right past them. The same is true of *Project A-Ko* (1986) and *Martian Successor Nadesico* (1996), which are both filled with

City Hunter (TV, 1987–97) is a kind of private-eye or gun-for-hire show; its competent and athletic but uncontrollably lecherous hero gives the viewer both action and laughs. Even Jackie Chan did a live-action version of *City Hunter* (best seen after you are famil-

LUPIN III The theater program book for the *Castle of Cagliostro* movie, which features the popular Lupin character.

good action. (There is also a *You're Under Arrest* TV series that appropriately begins with episode 5.)

Science fiction police shows range from the humorous character-focused *Mobile Police Patlabor* (1988–92) to *Dominion Tank Police* (1988–89) with its heavily munitioned and out-of-control police force applying techniques of armored warfare to urban crime control.

A more realistic crime drama is the *Sanctuary* movie (1995). Its tale of gangsters and corrupt politicians does a good job of animating a segment of the much longer manga series. A story of politicians and gangsters, it offers plenty of sex and violence in an interesting storyline.

Romance

Romance, often in the form of romantic comedy, is a theme of many anime. It, of course, can also be a significant factor in many shows from other genres, such as *Blue Seed*, *Ranma 1/2*, or *Gundam 0083*, where it motivates the actions of characters in the stories, just as love motivates human behavior in every time and culture. The two best-known TV "pure romance" series are *Maison Ikkoku* (1986–88) and *Kimagure Orange Road* (1987–88) with

iar with the anime, or you won't get most of its jokes). Then there is *Gunsmith Cats* (1995), a series about a female bounty hunter who is also is a gun store owner. Set in Chicago, it is heavily based on 1970s American action movies.

The four *You're Under Arrest* OVAs (1994–95) are about a pair of female traffic police officers and the staff at their station, and it provides laughs, excellent animation, drama, and, again,

YOU'RE UNDER ARREST MOVIE Yoriko and Aoi prepare to fight. Note: these arms are not standard issue for the Japanese police.

drawing you in and making you want to see the next episode.

Girls' shows

Japan's traditional emphasis on separate roles for males (warriors and bosses) and females (mothers and homemakers) has helped create a significant market for anime and manga aimed at girls and women. Women play a major role in the industry as writers, artists, and animators—far beyond what is seen in other countries—and this shows in the kinds of programs being made. One of the most well-known examples of such a TV program is *Sailor Moon* (1992–97), which attracts viewers far older than its intended audience of young girls. The successful four-woman manga writing team of Clamp has been the source of many girl-oriented manga (shōjo manga) that have been adapted into anime, such as *Clamp Campus* (1997), *Magical Knight Rayearth* (1994–95), and *X* (1996). Other popular anime that came out of shōjo manga include the above-mentioned *Fushigi Yūgi* and *Revolutionary Girl Utena* (1997), the latter being perhaps one of the most alien anime from the perspective of conventional U.S. entertainment. *Revolution-*

their love triangles—or, better, love polygons—and dramatic stories of characters coping with feelings and circumstances. *Maison Ikkoku* was aimed at an adult audience not because of its sexual content but because its slow pacing and involved story would be too boring for kids. *Kimagure Orange Road* is both lighter and more dramatic, and it packs a punch with its depiction of teen hopes and anxieties. Both of these series are extremely adept at

KARESHI KANOJO NO JIJŌ Known among fans by its Japanese title, which roughly translates as "The Situation of He and She," this is an unconventional romance from Gainax that began running on Japanese TV in 1998. Here Sōichirō and Yuniko share a tender moment.

ary Girl Utena is an extreme example of shōjo storytelling, with its quasi-European architecture, elongated chara, and highly abstracted plot. Even so, many have fallen in love with this most unusual school drama, even guys.

MAGICAL GIRLS

"Magical girls" is the term applied to the subgenre of girls' shows that feature a girl chara who has supernatural powers or possesses powerful magic objects. A major subgenre of the magical girl subgenre has as its main character a girl who obtains an object giving her the ability to transform into a superheroine, sometimes with an adult or teen body. Such fantasies of maturation and gaining power are un-

derstandable among young girls and have long been a part of many childhood games, such as playing house, and of girls' adventure stories. And of course magical objects are desirable to toy manufactures, who can then make replicas for sale.

One of the sweetest of the magical girls shows is *Card Captor Sakura* (1998–2000) in which a girl has to recapture a set of magical cards she has unleashed on the world, all the while coping with her own not-so-magical daily life.

Parodies of the magical girl genre can be seen in the *Pretty Sammy* OVA (1995–96) and TV (1996) series, where the young girl does not take on an older body but still gains powers to fight against evil foes with the help of an animal sidekick. In *Otaku no Video*

REVOLUTIONARY GIRL UTENA Utena, the title character of this series, prefers to wear a boy's uniform at school.

LESSONS FROM OTAKU NO VIDEO #4

Misty May in her transformed state. Normally she is just a shy school girl, but with the powers of a magic wand she turns into an older looking chara in a sequence that is a reference to the manga and to the anime chara Cutey Honey. Her two lion cub companions are Posiking and Nega-king. The bunny-suited Misty May chara herself is a reference to an anime short worked on by some of the founders of Gainax for the 1983 Daicon IV science fiction convention's opening ceremony. The two cubs are references to another mascot named King, Nadia's sidekick in Nadia: Secret of Blue Water, a TV anime also done by Gainax.

there is an anime within the anime in which a schoolgirl transforms into the busty, bunny-suited Misty May. May has *two* animal sidekicks, mascots being a staple of such shows.

Strong female chara are not limited to shows intended primarily for girls. Many strong girls and women also appear in shows designed for a male audience. Examples of such chara include the Dirty Pair, the heroines of

Bubblegum Crisis, and Noa Izumi of *Patlabor.* Japan has a history of strong women in literature, legend, and society. In the postwar era, women have come to play a significant role in public office both at local and national levels. The Japanese government has also promoted policies encouraging women to be more active in business and society, and these policies at times are reflected in the TV programming of NHK.

Boys' shows

Boys' shows have traditionally emphasized action and machinery. This is very evident in the giant robot shows of the 1970s and in *Mach Go Go Go* (*Speed Racer*) of the 1960s. The appeal of these shows comes not just from the abundance of technogadgets, but from the dramatic situations with heroes that science fiction lends itself to. What, after all, is a better setting for action drama than a world of super-weapons or the frontiers of outer space?

MARTIAL ARTS

Just as girls have their Magical Girls shows, boys have their martial arts programs that feature endless series of

©1996 SUNRISE /TX

THE VISION OF ESCAFLOWNE The young king and warrior Van with Hitomi.

Today the gender divide has become more nebulous with the appearance of shows like *The Vision of Escaflowne* (1996), which combines a strong design for the girls' characters with lots of mecha action that boys like. Another example would be *Gundam Wing* (1995), with its mecha action and the important role of the charas' feelings.

Sports

fight scenes and lots of other male-bonding opportunities. One example, seen recently on American TV, is *Dragonball* (1986). Then there are the continuing slugfests like *Fist of the North Star* (1986), as well as several anime based on fighting games such as *Street Fighter* and *Fatal Fury*.

Crossover shows

The divisions between boys' and girls' entertainment are not as clear as they used to be. Sure, there have always been shows that appealed to both boys and girls, but in the past there were also shows that strictly aimed at one sex or the other. These programs had strong stylistic elements that clearly identified their target audience (and perhaps drove the other sex away).

One genre not found much in animation in the West is sports. In sports shows games and athletics are the focus of the lives of the characters, whose activities on the team (for these shows usually involve team sports) play a major role in their interpersonal relations. Few of these shows have made it to America, although several are of excellent quality. *One Pound Gospel* (1995), a story about a failing boxer and a novice nun, is one of the few sports anime that has been translated; most likely this is because it was based on a manga of the same name by the famous Rumiko Takahashi, author of the best-selling *Urusei Yatsura, Ranma 1/2,* and *Maison Ikkoku.*

One series that was very popular in Asia is *Slam Dunk* (1993–96), the tale

©1997 REX ENTERTAINMENT

PERFECT BLUE Mima in a very tense moment in the story.

of a high school basketball team. Now I hate basketball and love *Slam Dunk*. You can't help but enjoy this story; the game is simply another arena where the chara have the opportunity to interact.

Adult shows

When I say "adult" I'm not talking porn. I mean shows that are aimed at older audiences and make kids fidget and leave the room out of boredom. *Maison Ikkoku* is a great example, with its long novel-like structure and often slow-paced story. More action-oriented shows can also fall into this category, like the first two *Patlabor* movies whose big action at the beginning and end frame a leisurely yet suspenseful middle. *Perfect Blue* (1998) is an anime few non-adults would like because of its very complex storyline; even experienced moviegoers need to pay close

attention or they'll miss significant plot points.

LITERARY ADAPTATIONS

Related to adult shows are animated versions of literary works, like the titles in the *Animated Classics of Japanese Literature* series made for TV broadcast in the mid 1980s. Among these are *The Priest of Mt. Kouya* by Kyōka Izumi, *Izu Dancer* by Yasunari Kawabata, *A Ghost Story* by Yakumo Koizumi (pen name of Lafcadio Hearn), and *Voice*

©1987 ASAHI GROUP / HERALD GROUP / TAC

TALE OF GENJI The cover art for this anime adaptation of part of the famous novel.

48

©1988 AKIYUKI NOSAKA / SHINCHŌSHA

GRAVE OF THE FIREFLIES In the devastation near the end of World War II, many children had to fend for themselves when their parents were killed.

CHRONICLES OF THE WAR

A significant subgenre of literary adaptations includes works related to World War II. Many Japanese writers have produced essays, novels, and autobiographies based on their wartime experiences. In 1988, Studio Ghibli released the tragic *Grave of the Fireflies,* based on an autobiographical novel about two orphans near the end of the war. Also available in English is *The Rail of the Sta*r (1997), based on the memoirs of a Japanese woman who spent the wartime years as a small child in Korea. Many of these wartime adaptations present the world through the eyes of innocent children at a time when the right wing and military were directing the policies of the Japanese government.

from Heaven by Jiro Akagawa. All are absorbing and very well done.

Older literary works have also been adapted into anime. A portion of Lady Murasaki's 11th-century story of love and court intrigue, *The Tale of Genji,* was animated in 1987, and the massive 19th-century warrior epic *Nansō Satomi Hakkenden* (Satomi and the Eight Dogs) by Bakin Takizawa was adapted as an OVA series under the title *The Hakkenden* (1993–94).

Gay themes

Anime with a male homosexual theme also exist, but on a small scale. Most stories about gay men have a largely *female* audience in Japan, and these women generally prefer manga formats such as those featured in magazines like the popular *Juné.* (There are also anime with lesbian themes, with the explicit ones generally aimed at a *male* audience.)

Often anime will use a gay or lesbian character to add color to the story; depending on the show, the portrayal can be a serious, comedic, sympathetic, or degrading. Most such characters are used for comic effect, as in the first *El Hazard* OVA (1995) series (which I highly recommend) with Alielle, a delightful and impressionable young woman whose unwanted attentions make some of the other female characters nervous, to our amusement.

Sympathetic gay chara can be seen in the figure of the policeman Daley in the original *Bubblegum Crisis* OVA series; a better example might be the major character Noriko in *Fushigi Yūgi*, whose love for the emperor caused him to pass himself off as a woman so that he could gain entrance into the imperial palace.

Hentai

Although some people still associate anime with sexually explicit materials, X-rated or adult material in fact represents a very small fraction of the totality of anime production. Porno titles are almost all made for the OVA market since they cannot be shown on TV, and theatrical distribution is likewise not very large.

Adult genitals and pubic hair are usually only shown in pornographic anime or manga, and even then but rarely. In the past, strict Japanese censorship laws were such that genitals were either not shown at all or were covered over in manga with a black dot and in anime with large fuzzy areas or digitized pixels. Recent changes in Japanese laws allow more explicit images to be used not only in adult anime and manga but also in photography and film. This trend is only slowly showing up in material available in the U.S. (Some of the older titles were made with minimal attention given to the genitals, since animators knew that these would be covered by a digital matrix when the duplication masters were made. But when these titles were released in the U.S. the censoring was simply not added, giving American viewers a glimpse of some rather sketchy-looking privates.)

● ●
Hentai

A complex Japanese word, hentai in the context of anime means perverted or pornographic. Sometimes the word is simply written and pronounced in abbreviated form as the Roman letter H, which is pronounced in Japan as "etchi."

© 1992 T. MAEDA / DAIEI

LA BLUE GIRL Miko Mido is a ninja heroine.

from there into anime. All of this simply means that there is a broad range of story types in hentai anime, as complex or as shallow as in other genres. Hentai anime titles include the comedic sex-and-tentacles ninja stories of *La Blue Girl* (1992–94). Stories with a gender-bending theme and a more serious message can be found in such anime as the *Countdown* series (1995–96). Then there is *F3: Frantic Frustrated and Female* (1994–95), about a young woman's continuing attempts to achieve orgasm, often with the help of other women.

• •
Sailor fuku and the law

The sailor suit is a common style of girls' uniform for middle and high school students. The design comes from European sailor uniforms and was introduced in the early 20th century.

As is the case with many other genres, porno anime are mostly adaptations of manga aimed at the adult market. Some X-rated anime are based not on manga but on pornographic video games (in fact, most of the images posted to the alt.binaries.pictures.erotica.anime newsgroup are not from anime but from games or manga). Several tasteful erotic manga in Japan are made by and for women, so there is a very non-Western, non-male-centered view of the erotic that enters into some of the stories, and

In the U.S., fear of being charged with promoting child pornography or of the possible passage of laws outlawing drawings of minors in sexual situations has led several U.S. companies to up the age of anime characters so that high school girls now become college students. A simple guideline here: if a girl chara is wearing a *sailor fuku* (sailor outfit) or any other school uniform she is too young to be a college

LESSONS FROM OTAKU NO VIDEO #5

When Kubo first visits Tanaka's fan circle, one of the items we see in the room is this *sailor fuku*, wrapped in a plastic dry-cleaning bag on the wall. The boxes stacked next to it are all various model kits, mostly from anime and science fiction shows.

student. College students don't wear uniforms.

Press coverage of sex and anime

In any discussion you may have with others, it is important to remember that the English-language press has often made statements about sex in anime and manga that are just plain untrue. One dramatic example is when the character Belldandy in the *Oh My Goddess!* anime was referred to some years ago as a "soft porn goddess." *Oh My Goddess!* is actually a very tender romantic comedy; Belldandy does kiss

her boyfriend a couple of times, but not on the mouth. Her trendy sister Urd is a bit outrageous, but strictly for comedic effect and only in one scene.

One result of this false reporting is that some video stores have classified all anime as "for adults only," even sweet titles like *My Neighbor Totoro* or kids' shows already on American TV like *Dragonball* and *Sailor Moon*.

Congress strikes back!

A few years ago a bill was submitted in the U.S. Congress that would have made it illegal to represent the buttocks of any underage character or the breasts of any underage female in any medium. Imagine parents being arrested not only for child pornography but also for child abuse for having a copy of the first episode of the *Ranma 1/2* TV show or of *My Neighbor Totoro* for their kids!

The best place to get good, solid information on this subject is *The Erotic Anime Movie Guide* by Helen McCarthy and Jonathan Clements. For details on this and other anime-related books, see chapter 10.

FOUR

WHAT MAKES ANIME UNIQUE?

There are many factors that make anime such a distinctive form of visual expression. Some of these have less to do with art style than with the way the industry has developed over the years. While anime grew in Japan, regular domestic cinema dramatically declined as a result of competition from foreign films and the popularity of home video. The economic good times of the 1980s did much to make funds available for anime as well as to create a market for related merchandise. And much of the look and feel of anime is the result of its ties to manga, a very significant entertainment industry in its own right.

Historical differences

There are a number of important structural differences that distinguish the animation industries in Japan and the United States. Most notable is the large number of animation studios in Japan, many of which function as subcontractors for larger companies. Japan also boasts a massive comic book (manga) industry, beside which the anime market pales in comparison. Manga is a major source for anime stories and provides tested tales that have already established an audience; many manga publishers in Japan have their own anime divisions or special relationships with studios to develop their works into films.

As a result, Japanese animators not only have a large body of stories to draw from, but lots of competitive pressure that encourages them to experiment in order to reach niche markets.

In contrast, in the U.S. a handful of large players—Disney, Fox, and Warner Brothers—completely dominate the market. Controversy over story content in the 1950s led the comic book industry in the U.S. to self-censorship, hampering mainstream growth and, until recently, relegating the product either to kid's shelves or a slightly unsavory "underground." It is still hard to find regular comic books (as opposed to more literary graphic novels) in U.S. bookstores, and American comics shops themselves have fallen on hard times.

In the U.S., the studio product over the last few decades has been much more homogeneous, in many cases well made but less daring, and certainly not breakthrough enough to build new audiences. Theatrical-release musicals with lots of slapstick only have so much appeal. The same is true of simplistic hero vs. villain TV fare. The problem with studios repeating successful formulas of the past is that the product rapidly gets boring.

Anime companies

Making anime is a complex process. Check the credits of an anime and see how may different companies are involved. For example:.

From: *Catnapped* (1995)
Oh Productions
Studio Junio
Studio Boomerang
Mushi Production
Mad House
Studio Hibari
Production I.G

From: *Ghost In The Shell* (1996)
Production I.G
Group Donguri
Studio Takuranke
Studio Junio
Studio Wombat
Phoenix Entertainment
Tezuka Production

From: *Cowboy Bebop* (1998)
Studio Cockpit
Studio Takuranke
Studio Deen
Anime World Osaka
Maki Pro
Asahi Production

Many of these companies are familiar names among fans, and some are so well known that they have their own followings of fans who will watch titles just because they worked on them. For example, Mad House and Production I.G are very well respected for many of the titles they have helped create. Some companies are big enough to produce their own titles and take on extra work in slow times, or are subdivisions of major companies that do subcontracting as part of their regular work.

Story qualities

A few years ago I spoke with my nephews hoping to find out some of the things they liked about anime as compared to American animation. What they said they liked is that anime often has a story told over a long series, that you can never be sure what the ending will be, and that it is not unusual for a major character in an anime or manga to die, to lose the one they love to another, or to fail at what they are trying to do. Even in works aimed at children these things happen. My nephews felt that American animation endings were just too sappy and predictable.

Another thing my nephews liked in anime was that the characters are more complex. Anime villains can be understandable and even change their ways; heroes can show bad traits and even commit horrid acts, though they regret them. Of course the "little guy" nephew also said he liked "cool robots."

Now much of my nephews' view is probably due to their having seen a good amount of the highly dramatic *Mobile Suit Gundam* saga. But their comments can apply to many other anime. The long narrative structure of much of TV and OVA anime—with a beginning, middle, and end to multi-episode series—is a clear departure from much of English-language TV. The unpredictability of plot in many shows as well as the more complex characters in better anime can quickly lure viewers in and keep them watching.

Some Americans have trouble with what I call the "Shakespearean quality" of anime and manga stories. In a serious anime there can be a sudden comedic interlude; in a farce, there can be tragic moments. For example the first *Patlabor* movie is fairly serious, but when Shinohara has an argument with the commander it gets pretty funny; and in *Fushigi Yūgi*, a lightly humorous series, some of the secondary characters die. Theater lovers should find this not strange at all. *Romeo and Juliet* does not end well for its star-crossed lovers, but along the way it has some pretty funny moments. If it works for Will . . .

The human element

In anime the feelings of characters play an important role in shaping their actions, much more so than in most American products, live or animated. This is of course true in romantic shows like *Maison Ikkoku* or *Kimagure Orange Road,* but it is also important in action-oriented shows, even among the minor characters. Now what viewers may find interesting is that rarely do the characters speak about their feelings; instead they act from what they are feeling, expressing their emotions

©1995 MASAMUNE SHIROW / KODANSHA / BANDAI VISUAL / MANGA ENTERTAINMENT

GHOST IN THE SHELL Batou next to Motoko, after they have captured a fugitive.

in actions. After all, words are just words unless backed up by deeds. Kubo in *Ranma 1/2* professes love and passion to more than one female character, but his behavior is insincere. Ranma does not profess such feelings toward Akane, but as the series goes on he acts more affectionately.

A common, related theme is that of the man who cannot express his feelings in words, or is not even sure what his feelings are, but nevertheless takes action. Witness the behavior of Batou in *Ghost in the Shell* toward Motoko or Ken toward Miyuki in *You're Under Arrest*. Both have trouble clearly stating their feelings and struggle to express themselves to the one they love. It is not just men; female characters can also hold back or be confused by their emotions, as in the case of Madoka in *Kimagure Orange Road* or Kyoko in

Maison Ikkoku. Madoka and Kyoko come to realize their feelings, but it takes the possibility that another woman will get the man they love to finally make them speak what they feel. Having some characters who are not really sure about their own feelings adds greatly to the story, as the characters need to work out within themselves what they are feeling and then have to make a decision on how to act toward others.

Japanese culture in anime

Pay attention when you are watching anime and you will see many fascinating Japanese cultural details, from *shōji* screens to Buddhist bells to people taking off their shoes when entering a home. Japanese elements are of course rarely seen in Western animation (full as it is of its own cultural details and assumptions). In my book *The Anime Companion: What's Japanese in Japanese Animation?* I identified many specific Japanese cultural details in anime that I could locate solid information on.

But there are many broader aspects of Japanese culture and society not covered in my book that are worth noting. For example, there is the motiva-

©1995 GAINAX / PROJECT EVA / TV TOKYO / NAS

NEON GENESIS EVANGELION Shinji holds an injured Rei during an attack on Tokyo III in the first episode of the series. He is about to make a decision that will determine the direction of his life, and perhaps that of all humanity, a decision to perform actions he had rejected just moments before. It is just this type of scene that made adult viewers pay more attention to this series.

tion to succeed or to do the right thing for one's elderly parent. There is Japan's emphasis on feelings, or the bittersweet sense of time's passage as indicated by a falling leaf or cherry blossom. A character may react badly to a poor grade on a report card, or struggle for a good grade on a high school or college entrance exam as in *Birdy the Mighty* (1996) and *Maison Ikkoku*.

There are many traditional character values portrayed in anime that Japanese (and Western) parents find attractive, such as perseverance, sincerity, and determination in the face of adversity. There are also particular Japanese words or speech patterns that are not easily translatable yet add an element of subtlety. For example, one chara may address another as *senpai* (senior). The word possesses such an abundance of meaning in terms of defining the relationship between the characters that in the *Kimagure Orange Road* TV series the subtitlers decided to leave the word untranslated, with only an explanation in the liner notes.

● ●
Senpai

Generally the word senpai means someone with greater seniority in a particular situation. Often the word is used in reference to an upperclassman in school. The person who is the junior in this relationship is called the *kōhai*.

Cinematic effects

I have heard it said that many people who work in the anime industry would rather be doing live-action movies. The great number of cinematic effects used in anime supports this idea. Much of the action in anime is framed as if it had been filmed with actual cameras. In fact, a book on cinematic effects could easily be illustrated just with images from anime, even images from a single show.

American animation is still largely

YOU'RE UNDER ARREST These images from the OVA opening show a complex sequence done as if it was one long shot from a camera. Such a shot in reality would involve some very complex camera boom work.

based on stage plays, with a static background that the characters move in front of. There are exceptions of course; some of the more expressive episodes of *The Simpsons* do have dynamic backgrounds. But, overall, Japanese backgrounds are more likely to be in motion and to change and turn. Obviously, this costs more money, which is why a lot of American studios avoid the effect. Not all anime uses a dynamic background, but much of it does, along with other cinematic effects like pan shots, angles, distance shots, scenes where the focus between the foreground and background changes, and so on.

The historical roots of such effects are in the 1950s and the manga of Osamu Tezuka. Tezuka was a great fan of American films and animation, including the works of Max Fleischer and Walt Disney, and his manga were rich with elements that could have been lifted straight from a movie theater. Tezuka's dynamic illustration style and pacing is cited often by later manga artists as what drew them to his work when they were children. Tezuka later incorporated his cinematic drawing style into his own films, so it is fair to say that anime's cinematic elements originally came not from cinema but, in a roundabout way, from manga.

Timing and editing in anime are also different from what we are used to in the West. Action in anime often takes longer to unfold, and there are many moments with no dialogue at all. Silence helps build atmosphere in a story. Compare the English redubbed and subtitled versions of Hayao Miyazaki's *Kiki's Delivery Service* and you will time and again hear additional lines spoken or just verbal sounds at moments that were nonverbal in the original.

Another difference between American and Japanese animation is that in Japan the anime is filmed and then the voices are added (or at least the storyboards are done and the voices are recorded while the animators are at work). In the U.S., the voice actors are recorded first and only then is the animation created. An example of this is seen in the first *Martian Successor Nadesico* episode. Japan's way of working occasionally results in the lips not quite matching the words; sometimes this is caused by a last-minute

change in the script. Of course there's not much you can say about American reviewers who have on occasion complained about the words and lips not being in synch when reviewing anime redubbed into English. . . .

Visual conventions

Anime's visual conventions are not just limited to obvious cultural details but are unique stylistic ways of communicating and expressing feelings and ideas. I'll describe a few of these here.

LARGE EYES
Everyone who sees Japanese anime and manga comments on the fact that the characters's eyes are not only large but also don't look especially "Asian." The large eyes come from the influence

BLUE SUBMARINE NO. 6 Mayumi's ferocious look is stronger due to the expressiveness of her eyes.

© 1998 SUNRISE

COWBOY BEBOP Fay Valentine is dressed for an evening out at the opera; the elongated shape of her eyes is a visual clue that she is not really all that innocent.

of early animation, especially that of Osamu Tezuka, who admired works of Max Fleischer Productions in Hollywood such as the *Betty Boop* and *Popeye* cartoons. Large eyes more easily express sadness, anger, happiness; the whole range of human emotion can be communicated through the eyes.

Large eyes are favored in a culture like Japan's that puts such a high value on "cuteness." Large eyes are often used to express innocence, and younger characters will often have eyes larger than those of the adults. In *Ranma 1/2*, for example, the characters Akane and Ranma have large eyes, but their fathers do not. Kuno the upperclassman does not have large eyes— but then Kuno is not only not innocent, he is a dangerous nutcase. In

girls' manga the size of eyes can get so exaggerated that a *Urusei Yatsura* OVA even spoofed the convention. In "Terror of the Girly-Eyes Measles" many uncute chara caught a disease giving them large pool-like eyes, much to the disgust of those around them.

HAIR

Hair is often an important stylistic element in anime. Again, this is due in part to the fact that so many anime are based on manga. A character's hair is one way of making him or her instantly recognizable, but because manga are published in black and white, there are few hair options: only shade (dark or light) and shape.

Most Japanese naturally have hair that is black or very dark brown; a very small percentage have a very dark shade of red. Imagine a black-and-white manga where all the characters have such typically Japanese dark hair; it would be hard to tell them apart. This is why some Japanese characters are "blond." These are actually characters whose "black" hair is done without shading in order to emphasize its shape and texture or just to make the character look different.

But what happens when a manga publisher uses a character on the color

© 1991 SOTSU AGENCY / SUNRISE

GUNDAM 0083 We get a good idea of the way hair moves as Chris gives Al a goodbye kiss on the cheek.

cover of a children's book or magazine? Here hair can take on bright colorful tones in order to catch the eyes of very young readers. A designer working on a cover for a kids' manga magazine may decide he wants a large bright pink, blue, or green area near the top of the cover and simply make a character's hair pink for that reason alone. The artist may then declare that arbitrary choice the "official" color of the character's hair, and this will be reflected in later anime that may be based on the original manga. Of course some characters have unusual hair because they are from another world, as in the case of Lum from *Urusei Yatsura.*

This manga hair style developed well before the modern fashion of bleaching and dying hair a light brown or of adding actual colors to make your hair look a bit like that seen in your favorite anime. A few years ago, during a discussion on Usenet, someone commented on how you don't see people with blue or pink hair on the street. I had to reply that I did, but then I live in the San Francisco Bay Area. However, I did note that at that time everyone with a solid color, rather than just a streak of color, seemed to be Asian.

Hair shape is also used to distinguish characters and make them recognizable. Some characters may have hair that is curly, natural, or permed, or that sticks out or clumps. This is somewhat unrealistic, as many Japanese schools have banned permed hair because of its associations with delinquency and to enforce a certain conformity among students (those with naturally curly hair may even resort to perming their hair straight just to blend in).

The movement of a character's hair is quite noticeable in anime. Hair flows in the breeze, moves when the character shifts suddenly, or comes to a halt. It gets wild during battle, and settles during a moment of stillness. A character may be pensive, with eyes cast downward, and a small lock of hair will come loose from behind an ear at a visually interesting moment. "Hair action" thus adds to the atmosphere of scenes and enhances the behaviors and feelings of the characters. It requires more complex cels and makes the anime more expensive, but the effect is a powerful one and adds much to one's viewing pleasure.

SWEAT DROPS

A recent visual convention indicating nervousness is to have a large drop of sweat appear on a character's head. This is not a small drop on the skin but a stylized drop, larger than an ear, on the side or back of the head depending on the perspective of the viewer. As with many visual conventions in anime, this probably has its origin in manga.

FLOWERS OR SPARKLES AROUND A CHARACTER

Another convention developed by Osamu Tezuka and often used in girls' manga is the appearance of flowers, sparkles, or abstract circles of pastel color around a character to indicate a love interest. The motif may adorn the chara, the person interested in the chara, or the two of them together,

GUNBUSTER Flowers and sparkles are used for humor as Noriko adoringly looks up to her senpai.

again depending on the perspective of the viewer. Roses with exaggerated thorns are used to indicate a dangerous love. This particular use of flowers and sparkles has been around long enough that it is often spoofed, as it is in *Gun-Buster* when we first see Noriko look at Kazumi, a senpai at her girls' school. Kazumi is surrounded by pastel circles and sparkles.

Japlish

English speakers are quick to notice the at times incorrect use of English in anime and manga. Many English words are customarily used in standard Japanese speech, and sometimes they are pronounced and employed in a manner quite different from their native use ("my-car," for example, was for many years an "English" phrase used in Japan as a noun to refer to one's personal automobile). English is also used for decoration and show. This is somewhat similar to the American use of French; pick up any woman's magazine and scan the ads for French snippets, some of them incorrect. Sometimes English is used in a punning manner so that readers of English can have an extra chuckle.

Violence

Much of the anime and manga translated into English features action or science fiction and fantasy. These genres in anime are usually no more violent than what can be seen in American comics, on TV, or in movie theaters. An important difference is that violence in Japan is often shown as having consequences. People actually get hurt, unlike in U.S. cartoons, where the person simply peels himself up off the pavement and resumes his life. But there are certainly cases where violence can be carried to an extreme; simply flipping through a few pages of a manga or checking the notes on a tape box will often let you know whether the material inside is suitable for children (or for you for that matter). Some non-Japanese anime companies have exaggerated the amount of violence or sexual content in their ads or box notes to encourage sales; the content of the material may actually be quite mild.

Nudity

Nudity is not unusual in anime and manga, even in TV shows and manga intended for children. Nakedness in

BLUE SUBMARINE NO. 6 Shocked from her fighting craft having been shot up, and gasping for breath, the water-breathing Mutio lies helpless on dry land.

Japan simply does not have the stigma or sexual innuendo it does in the United States. Often nudity is used for comic effect, and the characters involved may become highly embarrassed. Or a character may simply be taking a bath, as in the delightful children's anime classic *My Neighbor Totoro* when the father and his young daughters take a bath together, a normal and completely unsexual emotional bonding activity in Japan. On the other hand, sometimes nudity or partial nudity is used to sell the product, much as it is in the U.S.

Some would say that the Japanese are not concerned by nudity because mixed bathing is so common in Japan. Actually, mixed bathing among strangers is not so common in Japan anymore, although it is still practiced at some hot springs resorts. Just watch the *Ranma 1/2* bath scenes for examples of segregated bathing and characters reacting to intrusions on their side by members of the opposite sex.

Once when we were choosing a video to watch, a friend's very young daughter told me, "My mom says I can't watch anything with naked ladies." I replied, "But you watch Ranma." She looked at me like I was mentally deficient and said, "Those are girls!"

Sexual content

Given that some anime is released in the OVA format for specific market niches, it should not be too surprising that there is anime with highly sexual or pornographic content. The same is true of manga, which appeals to even more specialized adult markets. In the U.S. today, sexually explicit anime is quite overrepresented compared to the total amount of anime of all genres produced in Japan. Although this unfortunate fact has resulted in anime and manga being somewhat stigmatized in America, it really says more about the U.S. distributors' views of their customers than it does about the tastes of most Japanese fans and consumers.

FIVE

ANIME CONNECTIONS

In Japan anime is part of a wide spectrum of commercial entertainment that includes many other art forms and industries. When all the different sectors come together for publishing, distribution, broadcast, and merchandising, the result is a veritable juggernaut of creative work and aggressive marketing, producing tens of millions (or more) of both dollars in revenue and satisfied fans and consumers. While America has to date seen but one *Pokémon* wave, remember that in Japan there is not just *Pokémon* but many other shows, and they hit year after year after year.

The manga connection

Historically manga and anime go hand in hand. Most anime shows are based on popular manga. Titles available in the U.S. both as manga and anime include *You're Under Arrest*, *Ghost in the Shell*, *3x3 Eyes*, *Patlabor*, and *Gun-* *smith Cats*, to name just a few. In the late 1980s this began to change as some manga appeared based on TV shows or OVAs that were being released at the same time. But manga still has a much larger market than anime in Japan. It is cheaper to produce stories in printed form, and the diversity of the manga market makes it possible for artists and writers to experiment with all sorts of different characters and storylines. A series that proves its mettle in print has an excellent chance of drawing viewers to an anime version.

Far from being relegated to specialty shops and underground racks, manga are a ubiquitous fact of life in Japan, a form of popular literature that, in terms of pervasiveness and influence, is perhaps best compared not to comic books in the United States but to broadcast television. Manga is so popular that manga artists become major celebrities.

Manga in magazines

In Japan manga are almost always first serialized in magazines. These are not what most Americans think of as the thin, stapled Marvel or DC type of comic. Some of these magazines are really more like books, perfect bound and several inches thick, and many come out weekly. They may sell in the millions. While most magazines focus on a particular story genre—girls', boys', sports, and so on—all serialize several different stories by different artists in each issue.

There are many anime- and manga-related magazines available in Japanese and English.

Manga magazines are cheap, easy to obtain, and great reading for everyone from little kids to office workers. Many of these manga are read during the daily commute to school or work. Manga are not just restricted to special manga magazines, either. It is not unusual to pick up a computer magazine, say, and find a manga serialized in its pages, between the tech talk and the reviews.

Tankobon

Manga is first published in magazines, and then successful titles are collected together into books, in some cases hardcover editions. The Japanese word for such collections is *tankobon*. Once a manga story from a magazine is collected into book form it can easily comprise several separate volumes, as is the case with some of the long-running comedy and supernatural series of the talented Rumiko Takahashi or the adult political thriller *Sanctuary* (1993) by Fumimura and Ikegami.

Tankobon are where the publishers make most of their money from manga. Unlike the manga magazine, which is printed on cheap paper and quickly recycled, the tankobon gives readers a chance to buy their favorite series and read it again and again; plus, tankobon can be reprinted as long as the demand exists. And, of course, if a manga is made into an anime the tankobon becomes part of a whole merchandising spiral.

Latecomers to manga and anime, including most of us outside Japan, can obtain tankobon and read classic series from the past—assuming we read Japanese, that is (or we can just-look at the pictures). Many non-Japanese fans find manga a good way to practice their Japanese reading skills; my advice here is that you stay away from period manga with its archaic, more difficult Japanese, and choose a manga intended for younger readers, which will have *furigana* readings or pronunciations next to the *kanji.*

Kanji and furigana

Kanji are written characters—sometimes called pictograms or ideograms—that originated in China. In Japan kanji are used together with the phonetic scripts known as *kana. Furigana* are small kana placed next to a kanji to indicate its reading or pronunciation. They are most often used next to obscure kanji and in books, and manga, published primarily for children, who have not yet learned all 2,000 or so of the daily-use characters Japanese adults are expected to know. Reading Japanese manga is one way of practicing your Japanese without having to know the reading of every kanji, although manga language tends to be a bit slangy and full of jokes that are hard to decipher.

Dōjinshi

Not all manga in Japan is produced by commercial artists and publishers. Fans also produce their own works and gather them in what might be called Japanese 'zines, or *dōjinshi,* a word that suggests the idea of "publications among friends." There is a huge variety of dōjinshi publications and styles. While most are manga, some are heavy on text, including bibliographies and guidebooks. Today some dōjinshi circles even produce CD-ROM discs.

According to Fred Schodt in his book *Dreamland Japan,* much of dōjinshi production and buying is done by girls, as boys seem to have greater demands on their time to get higher grades and go to better high schools and colleges. The dōjinshi phenomenon has grown so big that there are now several conventions held throughout Japan, the most famous being the twice yearly Comic Market, commonly referred to as Komike.

Everything at these conventions is fan produced. It is often of very high quality. Pros who started as fans occasionally show up to keep in touch with their roots as well as show off stories rejected by their editors. The commercial companies and studios are represented by staff members who walk the aisles looking for new talent and perhaps by a few token promotional display tables. The larger cons can attract 400,000 attendees in as little as three days and have thousands of fans and fan groups selling their works (if they were lucky enough to be awarded table space in the convention lottery!). This scale is quite amazing when you consider that the largest U.S. comic convention devoted to professionally produced works draws just a fraction of that number of attendees. The cons in Japan are so vast and spread out that some fans even form buying squads; with maps in hand, and even radios or phones, they divide up the chore of buying their favorite titles in a very efficient manner.

Japanese companies don't worry much about their characters being used in most of the dōjinshi being produced. Trademark laws in Japan will protect their rights even if others produce stories with their characters, and Japanese culture tends to be more accepting of such fan homages than many other cultures. In the United States, anyone using copyrighted characters, either their likeness or just a text-based description, is in danger of being threatened with legal action. This supposedly happened to the fan authors of some alternative *Star Trek* stories in the 1970s; of course, it didn't help that some of their stories portrayed Spock and Kirk in an erotic relationship.

The sexy story is what many non-Japanese associate with dōjinshi, and there's a good reason for that. Such dōjinshi are the kind often sold at anime conventions outside Japan, and images from them are regularly posted to Usenet newsgroups devoted to erotic anime and manga. The underground nature of dōjinshi lends itself to exploring themes forbidden in commercial publications; all sorts of manga and anime works have been targets of sexually oriented parody, from *Neon Genesis Evangelion* to *Sailor Moon*. Even *Pocket Monsters* (known in the English-speaking world as *Pokémon*) has been the subject of an erotic dōjinshi. According to an article in *Manga Max* #5, rightsholder Nintendo called in the police after a thirty-two-year-old woman produced a very sexually explicit dōjinshi involving the cute character Pikachu.

But not all dōjinshi are sexual. Many are comedic parodies with characters in all sorts of situations or alternative stories much in the style of the originals.

Manga in the West

Manga translations are increasingly becoming available in the U.S. After starting slowly in the 1980s, English-language manga publishing has grown to the point that a children's manga translation, *Pokémon*, became the top-selling comic book in the U.S. in 1999. Issue # 1 was reprinted several times and sold over a million copies in less than a year and a half. These figures probably would have never been reached had it not been for the broadcast of *Pokémon* on U.S. TV.

Putting out an English-language translation involves not only translating the language but also redrawing the word balloons to accommodate the vertical Japanese text in a horizontal Western layout.

The most dramatic change involves page flipping. The Japanese traditionally read from right to left and open their books from what we in the U.S. would think of as the back. This means that panels in manga flow in a sequence that is the reverse of what we are familiar with. A story will begin at the top right of a page and then shift down and to the left as it moves along. When the manga is produced in English, all the pages need to be "flipped"

or reversed so that the image order flows instead from left to right. Flipping (or "flopping") creates some obvious problems, most of which publishers and fans tend to ignore or tolerate: right-handed characters become southpaws; cars have their steering wheels on the "wrong" side; and kimono are worn with the right lapel over the left in front, a style seen only when corpses are dressed for cremation.

Not all works in English have been flipped, however. The translations of *Ironfist Chinmi*, *Dragon Ball,* and *Five Star Stories* were published in the Jap-

The same two pages from *Neon Genesis Evangelion* in both unflipped and flipped (that is, reversed) formats. Shinji's face in the middle of one page gives you an idea of the differences in these layouts.

anese layout. Viz Comics employed both formats for its *Neon Genesis Evangelion* manga; the unflipped version, published at the same time, was titled "The Special Collector's Edition." And when Studio Proteus produced its *Blade of the Immortal* series—a left-to-right Western-style book—the designers went to great lengths to preserve the original layout and reduce the number of flops. This was no easy task, since manga are generally not laid out in neat square panels (which could simply be cut apart and re-arranged on a page) but in angled rectangles and jigsaw-like configurations that need to be completely refitted.

The 'zines shown here range from club newsletters to an English-language dōjinshi to full-blown magazines. They are only a few of the types of printed materials clubs or circles can produce.

Pseudo-manga

Pseudo-manga, also known as manga-influenced comics, are a growing phenomenon as more and more Western artists come under the influence of Japanese art and anime and begin to adopt its pacing and visual style in their works. Among the most famous and gifted artists working in this manner are Adam Warren (*Dirty Pair* and *Bubblegum Crisis*), Robert De Jesus (*Ninja High School*), Ben Dunn (also *Ninja High School*), and Stan Sakai (*Usagi Yojimbo*).

Some American comic book companies devote a significant percentage of their catalogs to such titles, most notably Antarctic, Dark Horse, and CPM Manga. Anime has also had some influence on other American media such as film. The makers of the movie *The Matrix* claim to have been influenced by the 1995 anime *Ghost in the Shell*, for example, but most fans consider the influence here to be very superficial, a borrowing of only a few minor elements of the sort that make anime and manga visually interesting.

Non-Japanese fanzines

Fan groups are always producing their own publications. Some fizzle out after a few issues, some last for years, and some even turn pro. The most famous English-language magazines with fan roots are *Anime UK*, *Animeco*, and *Protoculture Addicts*, all of which either started out as fanzines and grew into commercial publications or were offshoots of fanzines. Often such publications are club produced; this is a very good project for a club as it creates a centralizing activity for members and leaves a tangible record of club accomplishments.

The live-action connection

Non-Japanese are often unaware of the extent to which anime has a live-action connection, and this is no doubt because a lot of live-action programs are simply not available on video. *Kaijū*, or giant monster, films with famous creatures like Gamera or Godzilla have influenced or been parodied in some anime. In *Blue Seed*, for example, many of the Aragami, a type of angry spirit manifested as a curved gem, take the form of kaijū. There are also parodies of kaijū movies in some shows

GIANT ROBO Based on the manga of the same title by Mitsuteru Yokoyama, the *Giant Robo* anime was also a live-action show (1967) that was shown on U.S. TV as *Johnny Socko and his Giant Robot*.

such as *Mobile Police Patlabor* and *Kimagure Orange Road*.

Live-action shows remade into anime include *Super Atragon* (1995, based on the 1964 movie *Kaitei Gunkan*, which was released in the U.S. as *Atragon*) and *Sukeban Deka* (anime, 1991), originally a long-running TV series (1978–86) and then a series of movies (1987, 1988, 1992).

The live-action *sentai*, or team, show genre is already familiar in the United States through programs like *Power Rangers*. *Sailor Moon* is an example of such a team show done as anime rather than as live action. Other examples of live-action genres that have then been animated are many of the giant robot anime of the 70s and 80s.

SIX

HOW TO BE A FAN

OK, so now you have an overview of the anime basics, and you're thinking maybe you could be a fan. Or, you're already far along in your anime-fan career and are interested in hooking your friends in as well (at least that way you'll be able to borrow their anime and not have to buy everything yourself!).

But what does it mean to be an anime fan? What kinds of things do fans do? How long do their brains last? How large are their bank accounts? And do fans only hang out with other fans or does it just seem that way?

Watching the anime *Otaku no Video* is a good place to get an idea, even if a humorously warped one, of fan activities. Many fans think only of watching anime, but there is much more to do. Anime does not exist in an isolated world of its own. There is much to explore, such as manga, live-action movies, and trying your hand at drawing, cel painting, or model-kit building.

Anime is also a good introduction to Japanese culture, customs, and food. After all, how much of a fan are you if you have passed up chances to join your fellow fans in sampling *nattō* (fermented soybeans) or *okonomiyaki* (a grill-your-own pancakelike food)?

So get together with your friends and start exploring what you can do together.

Group activities

In Japan, the English word "circle" is used to refer to small fan groups who work on projects, such as dōjinshi, together. Many college campuses have clubs devoted to science fiction, and this usually includes anime. Japanese clubs play a major role in organizing large conventions, much as they do in the U.S.

In the U.S., clubs have been instrumental in spreading anime. In the early days of organized American fandom

LESSONS FROM OTAKU NO VIDEO #6

Tanaka's circle at work. Not only is there stuff all over the floor in this shot but other scenes in this section of *Otaku no Video* show almost every type of otaku activity. Included are model kits, animation cels, firearm replicas, magazines, uniforms (military and school), videos, manga, and various art supplies. Specialties of the members mentioned in Tanaka's introduction are science fiction, special effects, pro wrestling, *bishōnen* (pretty boys), alcoholic beverages, military matters, and games. There is one sleeping member, "off camera" in this scene, who does most of his work at night.

fore the screening, ignoring others who wanted to talk. Kids nowadays don't know how easy they have it. Why when I started out attending club meetings we had no access to projectors, we had to . . . Oops. Sorry for starting to sound like an old codger! I must say in my defense that I sure don't want to go back to those olden days.

In the 1990s clubs moved beyond organized screenings and conventions. Some began to produce their own, very illegal, subtitled versions of anime. Developments in multimedia technology now allowed you to take a translation of an anime voicetrack, with timing for when the chara spoke, put them on a computer, hook up an LD to the input, then output the translation and duped anime film to a VCR.

The resulting product would be a high-quality subtitled copy of an anime that was not commercially available in the U.S. Clubs would then share these copies with each other, introducing more anime to more fans who no longer had to struggle to read synopses in small text on bad photocopies in darkened rooms. Fandom grew rapidly. Some fan-favorite titles that were "fansubbed" in this manner and gained a significant following include

they provided access to anime in the form of tapes from Japan; often these had been taped from TV broadcasts. By the time they were shown at club meetings they might be several generations of copies removed from the original. At best, you had a photocopy of a synopsis to try to read in dim light as the video was played. Those who had struggled through such shows before tried to read as much as they could be

Kimagure Orange Road, Irresponsible Captain Tylor, Neon Genesis Evangelion, and *Rurouni Kenshin.* In several of these cases the fansub helped create a market for the later commercial releases.

FANSUB CONTROVERSIES

Since fansubbing is illegal, a loose code of ethics has developed to reduce potential conflict with the companies who produced the original anime or who are responsible for creating commercial import versions for sale in the United States and elsewhere. The "Fansub Code of Ethics" is a conventionally agreed-upon set of standards designed to prevent interference with the commercial activities of companies while at the same time making more anime available to more people. When I first heard of fansubs they were almost impossible to get unless you were a club. Individuals were largely out of luck. Today this has changed, but certain voluntary restrictions are still observed by most fansubbers and fansub distributors. Also, many owners of fansubs destroy their fansubs once commercial tapes are available, and some even buy the Japanese originals of fansubbed titles they own as an act of support for the original creators.

• •

The Code of Fansub Ethics (strictly interpreted)

A. A title will cease distribution in fansub form once that title is legitimately licensed for distribution in the U.S., even if that distribution may be far off in the future.

B. No cash for a fansub shall change hands; instead, the acquirer will send the fansubber a new blank tape and a self-addressed stamped envelope (SASE) so that the copied tape can be returned.

Starting an anime club

A great way to see a variety of anime is to attend the meetings of a local anime club. For a decade now I have been attending meetings of Cal-Anim-age Alpha, the anime club at the Berkeley campus of the University of California. Not only has attending showings transformed me from a novice hungering for every anime tidbit I could find into the obsessed viewer I am today, it has also enabled me to meet many other fans who have lots of knowledge in anime areas or genres I know little or nothing about.

If you attend a club, do whatever you can to help out, as there is always plenty of work to be done. If you don't have much time to help out, at least try to bring in new members by introducing anime to your friends and acquaintances and inviting them to meetings.

But what about those folks who live in areas where there are no anime clubs? Simple: start one! Now I said simple, but it is in fact not easy to set up and run a club that reaches a lot of people.

Here are some things you need to consider:

HOLD YOUR MEETINGS
IN A PUBLIC PLACE

You may, when you're starting out, find yourself watching anime in a den or family room with your buddies. But when forming a club, you'll find that meeting in someone's house won't work very well; your club will end up being mostly your friends, and you may have to deal with siblings and parents if you live at home.

If you are a student, find out whether you can use school facilities for your meetings. Schools often have AV equipment as well as space. You might also consider becoming an official school club with a faculty advisor. In grade and high schools this may be a problem, since attendance will be restricted to students and staff, and, de-

pending on school rules, screenings may be limited to times when the campus is open. College and University clubs are generally more accessible to the public with nighttime and weekend events. Also consider using your local public library, as libraries usually have a meeting room for public events and are often generous in allowing community groups to use them. Libraries usually have the equipment you need to show anime and may be able to help with publicity. You can also provide assistance to the library in return by helping them choose anime and manga titles for their collection (or even encouraging them to start a collection).

ROTATE OFFICERS TO PREVENT
STAGNATION

Many clubs are very small, due not to a lack of local interest in anime but to a kind of rut that it is easy for club officers to fall into. Club officers often run out of ideas and burn out from doing lots of work for the club. The worst thing that can happen to a club is for it to turn into a clique of officers and their friends; this not only gets boring but it also drives others away.

To insure that you rotate your officers, set up a system by which new officers join in as old officers step down or move on to new positions. This brings in fresh energy and ideas and prevents current officers from getting bored with the same jobs. Have enough officer slots so you can have a mix of new and old, thus ensuring stability and continuity. This is especially important with school clubs, as officers will graduate and leave, taking with them useful skills as the club struggles for survival. Be sure to train replacement officers who can step in if needed or help out during crunch times. Also, create lots of jobs and positions so there won't be too much work falling to just one person.

ADVERTISE, ADVERTISE, ADVERTISE!!!

A club is no good if it does not bring fans and nonfans together. The best way to let fans know who and where you are is to advertise. Make a list of contacts in the local media and send them notices regularly, well in advance of events. Make sure that your contact list is updated and that a copy is in the hands of at least one other officer so the club does not lose it if the person in charge of it leaves for any reason. Make fliers and see to it that they are distributed widely; have extra copies for people to pick up at meetings, or leave

LESSONS FROM OTAKU NO VIDEO #7

©1991 GAINAX / YOUMEX

Kubo, in his pre-otaku days, wanders through his school's festival. In the background is a booth set up by anime fans. The name of the booth is White Base, a reference to the ship in the original *Gundam* TV series. Other references to *Gundam* you will see in this scene are Tanaka dressed as Char Aznable and dōjinshi titles "Matilda Ajan" and "Artesia" (two female chara in *Gundam*). Setting up a table or booth at orientation events and school festivals is another way to bring in new members to your club.

them in local stores, coffee houses, libraries, and bookstores. And be sure to mention exactly where you meet; "100 GBP," for example, means nothing to someone unfamiliar with your city or campus. Spell it out as "100 Genetics Plant Biology Building, U.C. Berkeley."

SHOW A VARIETY OF ANIME

Not everyone has the same taste, so don't expect people to like everything that you do. In fact, don't trust people at all when they tell you what they find interesting. Anime has such variety and is so hard to categorize that people are constantly being surprised by what they find themselves watching. Someone who says they like dark stories about magic may hate *Bastard!* for its Heavy Metal rock references but love *Mahō Tsukai Tai!* for its comedic, light-hearted approach to the supernatural. Track down as many genres as you can and mix up the showings so that you don't have too much of one kind of anime at any given time. Some clubs show a lot of episodes for different programs at a single meeting; others show episodes from one program one meeting and from another the next.

One way to maintain attendance and variety is to show a few episodes from a single series after each scheduled showing; this keeps people coming back to sit through the scheduled title so that they can catch the next episode. Series that I have watched after scheduled showings include *Kimagure Orange Road* and *Slayers*.

Be sure to get permissions for titles that are licensed in the U.S. or in your country. Contact the licensing company and let them know what you want to show and the place and time of the showing. The company may even give you promotional items such as posters and videos that make great prizes for your members.

HAVE A NEWSLETTER

Create your own club 'zine or newsletter. This brings out the hidden talents of your membership, which may include writers, artists, and editors. One common approach is to release the newsletter in advance of each meeting with an article about the featured anime. Be sure to include all the proper copyright information with any images you use, including the names of the original Japanese company as well as U.S. company that holds the license. Some club members can coordinate the technical aspects of layout and printing, others can provide illustrations, and others will want to write about their favorite titles, directors, or other topics.

A newsletter can be used to provide background information about the club, news about the membership, details about upcoming local conventions and activities, editorial opinion about the anime industry, reviews of newly released films, and so on. A newsletter can also document the activities of the club and function as a sort of historical record of the growth of the anime community in your area.

CONSIDER NON-SHOW ACTIVITIES

BBQs and potlucks are a good way to bring people together to talk about anime, perhaps with a video on in another room for those who would prefer to just watch anime.

Shopping trips can also be fun in a group. Plan a route covering stores in your area that have anime and anime-related merchandise. This has the added benefit of supporting and promoting the local merchants who provide goods for fans.

You can even schedule educational events with speakers who are knowledgeable about anime and manga. This could be very useful for college and university clubs that often are seen as mere "entertainment clubs" by the school administration.

Get involved in conventions, in either a big or small way. There is always more work to be done.

Conventions

Anime conventions have become important regional, national, and even international gatherings for fans. Many anime fans use the Internet for communicating with other fans. Conventions allow us to talk face to face and strengthen ties as well as start new

LESSONS FROM OTAKU NO VIDEO #8

©1991 GAINAX / YOUMEX

Here we see Kubo painting an animation cel. This fan activity is often taught in workshops at anime conventions. In fact, I have seen such workshops in very large rooms filled with long tables and fans quietly, meticulously, painting cels. Kubo is just learning to paint cels in this scene and gets tips from Sato on how to deal with painting outside the lines.

projects and share information in a less structured way than the typed messages of e-mail and chat allow.

Conventions in Japan are a bit different from anime conventions elsewhere, as you might expect from anime's "home" territory. Conventions outside Japan have viewing rooms that often run twenty-four hours a day showing a wide variety of titles. In Japan the fans would already have seen almost everything of interest, so viewings are infrequent and usually feature new shows. Japanese conventions usually focus on specific areas of fan interest. At dōjinshi conventions, for example, fans get together to buy and sell their own publications and, nowadays, games and image disks.

Another fan magnet is the garage kit convention. Garage kit makers in Japan can obtain special licenses to make kits that will only be sold at specific conventions or for limited periods of time. This makes garage-kit conventions exciting, as fans attend looking for that special kit they know will not be obtainable in stores.

•••••••••••••••••••••••••

Garage kits

Garage kits are model kits made in very small quantities, usually a few hundred. These are made of cast plastic in a very labor-intensive method by small-scale manufacturers often working in garages, hence the name. Garage kits are generally manufactured by hobbyists for other hobbyists to buy.

Outside Japan, conventions are important places for fans to gather, talk, buy merchandise and videos, party, get silly, and have lots of fun. At a con you will find a dealers' room where vendors from around the country sell CDs, videos, posters, cels, model kits, figurines, and imported and domestic books. Prices for goods imported from Japan tend to be rather high, but this depends on the exchange rate, and

there is often a lot of haggling between dealers and customers, particularly at the end of the convention when dealers are most eager to sell. But if there is some CD or figurine you really care about, you should plan to get to the dealers' room early.

In addition to the dealers' room, at a con you will be able to go to panels and interviews featuring favorite artists, get autographs, attend workshops, question industry representatives, and, of course, watch a lot of anime.

Not that many years ago anime conventions in the U.S. were limited to a few localities on the West Coast and in the Deep South; then New England and the Rocky Mountain states started having cons. Today the number of cons has increased to the point that the large blank spots on the anime fan map are starting to fill in. Just about everyone in the U.S. now lives in somewhat close proximity to a con at some point during the year. Some of the major conventions held each year are Fanimecon (California), Anime Expo (California), Project A-Kon (Texas), and Otakon (Maryland). There are even genre-specific conventions, such as the Shoujocon held in New Jersey that specializes in . . . guess what?

I strongly recommend conventions for new fans. Just be careful and don't try to do everything at once. If you find your self hyperventilating, sit down and slowly enjoy a large soda to calm down. With this in mind I offer the following guide for con-goers to make their experience more comfortable, productive, and safe:

THE CON SURVIVAL GUIDE

1. Make sure you have accommodations either in the con hotel or at a hotel or motel close by.

2. Preregister for the con. No matter how long the prereg line is, the on-site registration line is much longer. Besides, if you preregister you usually get a cool badge. Preregistration information can be found on convention fliers and websites. These days almost every convention has a website.

3. Wear comfortable clothing, preferably something you can layer to deal with the differences in temperature between the outdoors, the hotel, and the dealers' room.

4. Check for schedule changes. Usually there are designated areas for postings or fliers that list location and time changes.

5. Locate hotel maps on walls and podiums. These can be handy when you are trying to find that location-was-changed-at-the-last-minute panel on sailor fuku recognition techniques.

6. Read the con rules carefully and abide by them. Many rules exist to keep peace with the hotel; remember: no hotel, no con.

7. Get proper sleep in each twenty-four-hour period.

8. Shower or bathe in each twenty-four-hour period at least once. I strongly suggest doing so in the morning and if needed again at mid-day. "Otaku Body Odor" is a recognized danger at some cons, and you should do your part to eliminate it.

9. Know where the bathrooms are in your vicinity. Even if you don't need them, someone else may need your assistance in finding them.

10. Eat regularly. Most cons provide a list of local eating places so you don't have to pay hotel prices for meals.

11. Stay hydrated. You don't want to be curled up in your room with a killer headache and nausea because you didn't drink enough water. This has happened to people I know.

12. Have cash for the dealers' room, as not all dealers will be set up for credit cards. Be aware that ATMs in the vicinity of cons rapidly run out of cash and are not usually refilled on weekends.

13. Expect to have to line up to get into the dealers' room. Many fans arrive early and wait for the room to open. But most cons have so many people attending that they need to restrict access to the dealers' room for fire safety, so you may end up waiting in the middle of the day too. Bring something to read while in line (a favorite manga or the con schedule perhaps?).

14. Don't stand around in the dealers' room having long conversations after you are finished shopping. Leave so others may enter.

15. Wait until the last day to buy easy-to-get items to make sure you have enough cash for the rarer items.

16. If you are attending a con outside your own country be sure you have the proper papers to get across the borders, both ways. Many U.S. citizens make the mistake of trying to get back from Canada with just a driver's license; if the immigration people are picky that particular day, you could find yourself spending an extra week in a hotel.

You will get a convention program when you sign in at the con. Find a place to sit down and go through the program book. There is so much to do that you can easily miss something unless you check the con program book carefully.

Cosplay / costume play

"Cosplay" is the practice of fans dressing up in the costumes of their favorite characters. Most of the costumes are homemade. (In Japan cosplay is so big that there are stores that specialize in tailoring and selling costume supplies, and there are also cons devoted entirely to cosplay.) Sometimes cosplayers form large teams, like the Eswat squad from the *Appleseed* manga at Fanime 2K. *Star Trek* fans do cosplay too, but there's a sameness to their identities. Anime fans have a distinct advantage here and can choose from dozens and dozens of popular chara, and not just those from anime but from manga and video games as well.

LESSONS FROM OTAKU NO VIDEO #9

The three anime chara costumes in this shot show a person dressed as Space Pirate Harlock, Kubo as Cobra, and Sato as Dominique Royal. Sato, in this and other scenes, seems to have a thing for outfits that show a lot of flesh. Otaku assignment: Identify all the cosplay outfits in *Otaku no Video*; use the pause button.

At U.S. cons there is always a capacity crowd at the masquerade. Here cosplayers make a variety of presentations, from simple walk-ons to real performances, both musical and theatrical. Parodies of favorite chara are especially well received.

If you plan to take part in the masquerade, check the con guidelines and rehearse so you don't go over the set time limits for performances. Learning to sew would also be helpful. . . .

Fan fiction

Where in Japan a fan or circle would create a dōjinshi, in the U.S. fans like to create "fan fiction," creative tales inspired by the plots and characters in favorite anime, manga, and video games. These can range from alternative stories that are very similar to the originals to off-the-wall take offs, including some that are very sexually explicit and not entirely respectable. Just add illustrations and you would have dōjinshi.

Fan fiction has become so popular that cons usually have fan-fiction panels presented by well-known fan-fiction authors. Some fan fiction can become very long and complex, with multiple chapters taking years to develop; if printed they would comprise many volumes.

With the long history of anime fan activity, it is not surprising to find that there are many fan fiction web pages. In fact almost all fan fiction distribution is done over the Internet these days. There is even a Usenet newsgroup devoted to anime- and manga-related fan fiction:

rec.arts.anime.creative

So if you are a fan looking for something to do beyond just watching anime, all you need do is look around and see what others have done, and are doing, and join in.

SEVEN

ANIME CONTROVERSIES

Every fan culture has its disagreements, and anime fan culture is certainly no exception. Spend some time haunting the anime newsgroups on the Internet and you'll find lots of "animated" discussion about specific titles, characters, and company practices. Some of these disagreements may have already reached the feud stage, with rival camps and factions vying for supremacy. There are no easy resolutions, since in many cases personal preference is all that matters (which I suppose is why these battles keep raging). Here's a brief overview of what anime fans are talking and raving about.

The sub/dub wars

A plague on many anime-related Usenet newsgroups is the constantly reoccurring flame war as to which is better, subtitled anime or redubbed anime. Like many "religious wars," this is a discussion with no real con-clusion as it is based purely on the preferences of each side.

A subbed anime preserves the original Japanese soundtrack and dialogue and provides English translations in subtitles. A redubbed anime replaces the Japanese dialogue track with a recording of voice actors in English.

Flame war

A term used for on-line discussions that either start out as or degenerate into seemingly endless arguments between two groups holding views that they have no interest in giving up. Some topics seem to turn up again regularly like bad pennies, such as sub vs. dub . . . or Mac vs. Windows.

Dub fans argue that it is hard to enjoy the images while at the same time trying to read the subtitles. Sub fans counter that you lose the original flavor of the film when you add English, and that most of the voice actors are pretty bad anyway. One such discussion I remember had a sub supporter laying out a cogent argument on how easy it was to watch the subtitles and still enjoy the images. The response from a person on the dub side was laced with personal insults and sneered that the sub proponent should just try watching some redub. The reply was simply along the lines of "I can't, I'm deaf!" Well, that flame war ended quickly.

My own take on this is more ecumenical: you decide what you like best. However, I must state that I do get irritated when a title I want is only available redubbed. I don't do Windows or redubs, so keep that in mind as you read this book.

DVD is eroding the need for such discussions, as most DVD discs contain both redubbed and subtitled versions of the anime on the disc. It is also interesting to watch redubbed anime with the subtitles display turned on to see the differences in the two versions.

Translation accuracy

Related to the sub/dub wars is the issue of translation accuracy. There are enough fans who can point out gross rewrites of dialogue in subtitled anime by simply listening to the original Japanese while reading the subtitles. These same fans will then raise the alarm and alert others to such bonehead gaffes in an attempt to embarrass the companies and translators.

With dubs, you are stuck with what you are given, and you might not know that there are significant alterations in the dialogue, even lines added that were not in the original, as was the case with *Kiki's Delivery Service*. Sometimes changes are made from necessity to match the lip movements, sometimes just to be cute, and sometimes to "improve" on the original (which is a little insulting to the original creators when you think about it).

Translators may use words that are roughly accurate in meaning but do not convey the nuance of what is being said; sometimes there is no good English equivalent (the word *senpai*, for example); and sometime the translator is careless, lazy, or incompetent. Kudos to the AnimEigo company, which took a more direct route with the subtitled *Kimagure Orange Road* TV series; it left out translations of a few "problematic" words like *senpai* ("senior"), *oniichan* ("big brother"), and *oneechan* ("elder sister") but took the effort to explain why in the video's liner notes. Now if companies would only stop referring to tanuki as raccoons I would be even happier.

Fifteening

A problem from the earlier days of anime releases in the U.S. is what the British call "fifteening." This is the addition of cruder language than was in the original, often to get a higher age rating and thus generate more sales. This is particularly annoying to those familiar with the original dialogue, as tough, down-to-earth, soulful characters end up sounding like cheap street thugs.

A recent example of this is in the English redub of *Princess Mononoke*. In the original Japanese, a character comments on the soup being watery. In the redub he says it tastes like donkey piss. Quite a feat, especially when you realize there were no donkeys in Japan at that time. This happens not only in redubbed anime but also with subtitled anime, though in the case of subtitled anime fans are quicker to raise a fuss.

The opposite can be true, with words being changed to make them milder, as in the case of *kuso* (shit) being translated as "damn" or "darn." In a scene at the end of the first *Gundam Wing* (1999) episode, a character tells Relena he will kill her; in the U.S. TV broadcast, this line was changed so that he says he will "destroy" her, a much different threat.

Dubtitling

Dubtitling is taking the same script written for the redubbed version of an anime and using it for the subtitled translation. Dubtitling is truly annoying, as the redubbed translation is often inaccurate when compared to what is being spoken in the original. The differences can be so extreme that for those who understand some of the original Japanese, watching a dubtitled anime can be very difficult.

Fortunately, dubtitling these days is a rarity, and fans are very quick to alert others when it does happen. You usually run across it with older titles that had previously been released on a dubtitled LD. In many cases, what was out on LD as a dubtitle has been properly subtitled for the DVD release. A significant case of a dubtitled release was Manga Entertainment's *Ghost in the Shell* LD; thank goodness the DVD has proper subtitles.

Cutting

It is not unusual for redubbed anime to have slower scenes cut to speed up the action. I once heard a vice-president of a U.S. anime company say that dub fans preferred low-brow action sequences, so atmospheric as well as slow moments could be trimmed to keep their attention. But, at the same time, he said his company would never do this to subtitled anime (the general perception is that fans of subs are more "purist" and would never tolerate this butchery). A quick check of running times between dubbed and subbed versions should help identify such cases.

There are other reasons for editing out material. In the encounter between Nagisa and Reina in *Here is Greenwood* (episode 2, 1992), one very short sequence of intimate touching was removed in the dub and left in the sub. In *Kite* (1998), the sex scenes were cut out of both versions, leaving us with some before-and-after scenes but a significant reduction in total playing time; no doubt this was done so the video could be sold to a lower age group.

American television still cuts anime for various reasons. Sometimes cuts are made to avoid cultural confusion,

HERE IS GREENWOOD Despite my mention of one unfortunate editing incident, this is a fun shōjo title about high school life.

©1991 YUKIE NASU / HAKUSENSHA / VICTOR ENTERTAINMENT / PIERROT PROJECT

but sometimes they are made because the U.S. producers think the show is just too slow. Most of the first episode of the *Vision of Escaflowne* was cut and spliced to speed up the action, losing much of the character development in the process. An episode of *Sailor Moon* involving tarot cards was not aired in the U.S. at all.

The most notorious cutting occurred with the redub of Hayao Miyazaki's masterpiece *Kaze no Tani no Nausicaä*, released in the U.S. in 1986 as *Warriors of the Wind*. Something like twenty minutes was cut, in-

THE BENEFITS OF CONTROVERSY

cluding almost all of the slower scenes that provided insights into the emotional background of the characters; what was left was a much shorter and more confusing action film, and a lot of outraged fans.

Mercifully, the contract for the U.S. rights to this title expired and was not renewed. Currently the Disney Company owns the rights, so we should see an uncut release of this classic within the next decade. Disney currently is being very slow in their releases of Miyazaki's Studio Ghibli titles, averaging one per year.

The Benefits of Controversy

If you are a relatively new fan of Japanese animation, you can see from this chapter that the history of anime in English has not always been a pretty one. So when you follow a thread on Usenet or listen to a conversation between fans, understand that what many of us had to put up with in the past makes us demand the best today. Anime fans are often a touchy bunch, demanding high quality in what they watch. This is one reason that anime fans were quick to adopt DVD with its

superior graphics quality. Fans also are quick to express even minor dissatisfactions with video releases; this keeps the companies on their toes and the quality of their products somewhat higher than they might be otherwise.

For example, if you compare Japanese cinema on video with anime on video you will immediately realize that anime is better translated and the subtitles are better timed in relation to the dialogue. There are two reasons for this: the high standards maintained by people in the U.S. anime industry and the pressure fans have and continue to put on companies to clean up their act.

Remember: as a fan you not only have the right to complain, you have the *duty* to complain. Just do it with some civility; clearly state your arguments and don't get drawn into flame wars.

The many controversies involving individual personalities and conflicts in the past are slowly being forgotten. I chose not to go into all these disputes here. People who made errors in the past should have the chance to move on to more productive activities, without being haunted by gossip over incidents that are over and done with and best forgotten.

EIGHT

ANIME STUFF

There is an astounding variety of anime-related merchandise available in Japan, and so much of it that the American tie-in industry—the Snoopy cups and Disney writing tablets—looks downright puny by comparison. Some anime shows generate so much related product that catalogs are made to document it all. *My Neighbor Totoro* and *Neon Genesis Evangelion* were both accompanied by large full-color books illustrating their related merchandise. There is even a large color catalog devoted just to books about *Gundam*, while other catalogs focus solely on *Gundam* models.

Not all anime produce this kind of volume, but even the minor tie-in lines are huge by American standards. Items are constantly going out of production to make room for newer ones. And steady sellers are constantly being redesigned and reissued. Perhaps the sheer glut of merchandise is the reason that there is no collectibles market in Japan comparable to the one in the US. In Japan, fans prefer to buy a few goods that they like rather than try to get everything or, worse, buy for "investment purposes."

Music

When you watch the production credits at the end of an anime you will notice that music companies show up again and again. In Japan, music companies produce the soundtracks to the shows in return for the right to distribute them on soundtrack CDs. Soundtrack albums in fact have been issued for almost every anime ever made in Japan. Since the music and soundtracks of popular shows can be very lucrative, the companies put in serious effort to produce good music. In the earlier days many anime soundtracks were rousing, often martial songs sung by male voices. Later, love songs by "idol" (popular teen) singers

stream record shops like Tower or Wherehouse. There have been some releases for the U.S. market such as the soundtracks for *Macross Plus* and *Ranma 1/2*. The albums you find can be classified into three broad areas:

OST, Original Soundtrack, usually the major songs or music from a soundtrack.

BGM, Background Music, often incidental short works used in a show.

Image albums containing music inspired by the story. The music on image albums is not necessarily from an anime but may be based on other, related media. For example, music albums have been inspired by the art book *Live: Noa Izumi Photographs,* a collection of drawings of the chara from the *Patlabor* series organized as if it was a photo album. Familiar examples of such music in the West include Ravel's (and Mussorgsky's) *Pictures at an Exhibition* and various "Music Inspired By" albums.

toro mer-
of garage
d a *Neon*
None of
or order-
tools for

alented composers employ symphonic music, jazz, rock, techno, folk, and just about anything else you can imagine, and they write for orchestras as well as small combos and solo performers. Their reputations have reached the point that fans will buy soundtracks for the composer alone, whether they have seen the anime or not. Joe Hisaishi, who has worked for Studio Ghibli, and Yoko Kanno, who works for a variety of companies, are two such composers with large and loyal fan followings.

Soundtrack and other anime-related albums can be purchased over the Internet or in some specialty shops in big cities. Very few make it into main-

There is also a type of instrumental "album" in which the music sounds like a wind-up music box.

The voices

Along with favorite shows there are favorite actors. Just as movie fans make it a point to see their favorite stars' films, anime fans follow the works of their favorite voice actors. Whole magazines like *Voice Animage* are devoted to them. Other magazines regularly feature articles about voice actors in their pages. Here are just a few of anime's top vocal stars.

Megumi Hayashibara has already had many roles, even though she just debuted in 1996, when she played a preschooler in episode 1 of *Maison Ikkoku.* Her parents would not let her pursue a risky career as a voice actress but were willing to let her do it as a part-time job while she was attending nursing school. By the time she graduated, her reputation was established (and she has never worked as a nurse). Add to all of this a weekly radio show and musical recordings both solo and with the groups DoCo (for *Ranma 1/2*) and the Takada Band (for *Blue Seed*).

A few of Hayashibara's more famous roles include Momiji in *Blue Seed*; Fay Valentine in *Cowboy Bebop*; Ayanami Rei, Ikari Yui, and Pen Pen (yes, the penguin) in *Neon Genesis Evangelion*; Chris MacKenzie in *Gundam 0080* (and *SD Gundam*); Ranma-chan in *Ranma 1/2* (she thought she was getting the Akane role); Lime in *Saber Marionette J* (and in *Saber Marionette J Again* and *Saber Marionette J to X*); Lina Inverse in the various *Slayers* programs; Achika in *Tenchi Muyo in Love*; and Ai in *Video Girl Ai.*

© 1997 REX ENTERTAINMENT

PERFECT BLUE In the opening sequence we see Mima singing when she was still a member of the trio Cham. *Perfect Blue* is an excellent example of the relationship between a quality soundtrack and anime.

Kikuko Inoue is often cast in soft-spoken roles such as Belldandy in *Oh My Goddess!*, Rune Venus in *El Hazard*, and Kasumi Tendo in *Ranma 1/2.* She has even played several roles in one show, such as Yoshiko Ueno and Misty May in *Otaku no Video* and Electra, Ikoriina, and the Narrator in *Nadia.* Not all of her roles are nice girls. She has also played the Panther in *Saber Marionette J*, Red Queen in *Miyuki-chan in Wonderland,* and nurse Ruko in *Ogenki Clinic.*

Yasuo Yamada is most famous for his portrayal of Lupin III, a role he played until his death in 1995. He was also a stage actor and regularly was the redub voice for Clint Eastwood characters when his American films were brought to Japan (after all, voice actors do more than anime). He even did the Japanese redub voice of King Arthur in *Monty Python and the Holy Grail.* An added touch here is that the Black Knight's voice in that film was done by Goro Naya, who also did the voice of Lupin's nemesis, Inspector Zenigata.

Trading cards

Sold in small packs, complete box sets, or included with videos, snacks, or other items, trading cards are a worldwide phenomenon—and they are found in Japan with an anime connection. Some of the anime-related cards are puzzle pieces that make up a larger image or have information on the back about a character, mecha, or item from the story, much as sports cards will have player statistics on the back. In Japan popular shows may generate several card sets over the years. While imported cards can be expensive, some U.S. companies, such as A. D. Vision and Pioneer include limited quantities of cards in their new video releases.

Phone cards

Related to trading cards are phone cards decorated with anime images. Japanese phone cards are not plastic cards with a pin number that you punch in when making a call. Instead, each comes with a certain preset value; you place the card in the phone slot and make your call, and the available credit on the card is reduced as the call progresses. Many companies use prepaid phone cards as promo-tions, and some promotional cards feature licensed characters as part of the design. Phone cards with anime images quickly became collector's items; some fans even refuse to make calls with these cards and instead store them away, kind of like record and comic collectors who never play or read their collections. Some U.S. anime companies have experimented with selling American-style phone cards, which use a PIN number, with limited success.

Stationery

Many shows, especially those popular with girls, spin off stationery items like pencils, erasers, notebooks, binders, and pencil boxes. These are not just bought by grade-school kids; young women and anime fans are a significant part of the market. I often carry a *You're Under Arrest* notebook, and my business card case has the logo from *Martian Successor Nadesico* on it.

Jigsaw puzzles

Jigsaw puzzles depicting scenes from anime are another part of the merchandising mix, but with an added twist; these are at times part of a larger kit that, when assembled, makes a fully functional wall clock with the completed puzzle filling the clock face. Many of the Studio Ghibli anime, most commonly *My Neighbor Totoro* and *Princess Mononoke,* have had such puzzles made from their images.

Toys

Some of the earliest anime and manga merchandise were toys based on favorite chara or mecha. These were often made of cardboard, tin, or cheap plastic. Nowadays the quality of materials and the sophistication of design is much improved, a reflection of Japan's advanced industrial might as well as of the fact that many consumers of these "toys" are in fact older fans with jobs and money.

CANDY BOX TOYS

A common source of cheap toys can be found in the candy racks of many stores. A few sweets in a box are accompanied by a simple model kit or toy; in fact, it is usually the toy that takes up almost all the space in the box. There is a huge variety of these little candy-box toys; they make a great gift for a small child and are cheap enough for kids to buy for themselves.

Often these are produced not by candy companies but by toy companies like Bandai, which issued a series of small candy-box model kits based on their popular *Gundam* series.

MODELS AND FIGURINES

With so many robots and mecha in anime, model kits are an obvious tie-in item. The toy giant Bandai has managed to make a small empire and a large amount of money off its *Gundam* kit line since the 1970s. In fact, *Gundam* models were sold in U.S. shops for years before the *Gundam* videos were translated and released commercially.

The Japanese have a reputation for producing model kits of very high quality. Anyone who has built Japanese models, be they anime related figures or cars and planes, knows that the craftsmanship is so good and the parts so exact that glue is often not needed to assemble them. Completed kits can often move in a variety of positions, and at times—as with the *Neon Genesis Evangelion* model kits produced by Bandai—there are even rubber parts cast on top of plastic joints, allowing for seamless moving segments.

One phenomenon in Japan is the garage kit, which I mentioned briefly

© 1991 GAINAX / YOUMEX

LESSONS FROM OTAKU NO VIDEO #10

The second part of *Otaku no Video* (released in 1992 as *1985 Zoku Otaku no Video*) opens with Tanaka mixing resin in a cup and explaining the manufacturing techniques of garage kits to Kubo. He pours the resin in the mold and starts the timer on his watch. Then the titles roll. After the titles we see Tanaka and Kubo waiting, staring at the mold. Tanaka's watch goes off. He pulls the two halves of the mold apart and displays a cast figurine. Kubo is in awe. This is the moment they begin their own company, Grand Prix, or GP for short. Who is the model for the figurine? There was an anime short worked on by some of the founders of Gainax for the 1981 Daicon III Science Fiction Convention's opening ceremony. This girl is the main chara for that piece, by the end of which we see her in the same captain's uniform used for the cast figure. There were actually casts made and sold of this chara by a real company named General Products, also GP for short. I was fortunate enough to find one at New Type, a small but famous anime model shop in San Francisco.

in the previous chapter. A garage kit is a cast model made in limited quantity, sometimes illegally without permission from the rightsholder, and at times in garages—hence the name. The quality possible with cast resin and vinyl is very high, since details can be included that just are not possible with injected plastic. But the molds wear out rapidly and the method is very labor intensive, so major manufacturers rarely produce cast kits, preferring to license the designs to smaller companies.

Ask permission to open the box before buying a cast kit. The best kits use a white resin; the resin of some older or cheaper kits may have a yellow or brownish color. (I have also heard of kits made with a wondrous, easy-to-work blue resin but have yet to see one.) Check for a parts list and make sure all the pieces are in the box. Check for bubbles in the casting, especially in undersides such as armpits; bubbles are a sign that the mold was wearing out. Some companies make copies of kits and sell them illegally; you may hear these referred to as "black box" kits (and the box in fact may be black). These kits often use inferior materials and have more flaws in the casting.

On the difference between injected and cast kits

Kits fall into two broad categories. Injected kits are the most common; any toy store will carry car and plane kits made this way. Cast kits, the other major type, are made in small quantities, often by hand casting.

Chara figurines are a popular type of garage kit since facial features and clothing require much more detailing. It would appear that Japan's centuries-old tradition of finely crafted dolls and puppets has simply been updated for garage kits featuring anime heroes and even actual persons. Fans like these chara kits not only for their great detail but because they can be dramatically altered. With some simple cutting and modeling one can reposition an arm, leg, or torso to produce a uniquely posed figure. Figures, by the way, are usually of female chara—perhaps because model kit assembling is primarily a male activity in Japan.

The most common injected kits are made by industry giants such as Bandai. But garage kits are produced in limited editions of perhaps a few hundred by many different small companies. It's fun to be in a store and stumble across a famous garage kit from a company that ceased to exist years ago. The downside of garage kits is that sometimes you find one that is almost impossible to build without both skill and dramatic modifications of the parts due to poor design by the kit manufacturer.

DOLLS

Dolls made to look like anime chara can range from a larger, more baby-doll style such as Arare from *Dr. Slump* to Barbie doll–like figurines with changeable clothing. There is even a market for featureless, poseable doll bodies that can be painted and altered to look like the chara of your choice.

PLUSH TOYS

Soft plush dolls are another popular category of anime-related merchandise. A fuzzy chara like the rotund Totoro is an obvious choice. But how about the small plush dolls of human chara in a chibi-bodied or superdeformed (SD) style, widely available as so-called UFO Catcher Dolls. UFO Catchers are those coin-operated arcade machines that have a crane you use to try to pick up a toy from a bin and drop it down a chute. The UFO Catcher Dolls are frequently modeled on some famous anime character. At first the dolls are available exclusively through such arcade machines; only after some time has passed can they be purchased in stores. This is done for no other reason than to encourage fans to spend money playing the machines. In the *Pretty Sammy 2* OVA, Sasami plays such a machine while waiting for her brother.

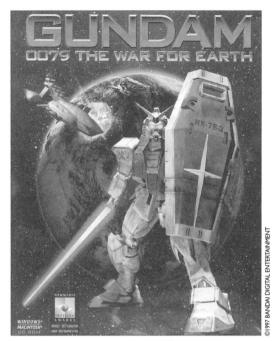

© 1997 BANDAI DIGITAL ENTERTAINMENT

GUNDAM 0079 THE WAR FOR EARTH cover art for the hybrid (Macintosh and Windows) computer game.

Chibi and SD

Chibi (small) bodied and Superdeformed (SD) are two humorous styles of representing chara in some anime and manga. Chibi-bodied refers to childlike bodies and superdeformed to bodies where the head takes up about a third of the height of the entire body. The introduction to the *omake* (extra) sections of *Blue Seed* uses SD-bodied chara.

Games

It used to be that video or computer games evolved from preexisting anime (which for their part had often evolved from earlier manga). Examples of this

pattern are the various *Ranma 1/2* and *Gundam* fighting or flight-simulation video games.

Today a game can spin off its own anime or manga. Some examples are *Sakura Wars*, *Final Fantasy*, and *Pocket Monsters* (*Pokémon*).

But the Japanese do not produce just a couple games relating to a few popular anime. They make dozens. In addition to the above-mentioned *Ranma 1/2* and *Gundam*, some examples are *Macross*, *Sailor Moon*, *Dragon Ball Z*, *Appleseed*, *Revolutionary Girl Utena*,

95

Serial Experiments Lain, and *Neon Genesis Evangelion*.

These are not all action games. Some include card or mah-jongg games with interactive chara, even strip poker or strip mah-jongg games where you can undress both female and male chara.

Board games and role-playing games are also popular. Several young children's shows have board games. The *Record of Lodoss War* was not only inspired by Dungeons and Dragons, but there is even a *Record of Lodoss War* D&D-style game in Japan. Other such games exist for *Tenchi Muyo*, *Silent Moebius*, and *Martian Successor Nadesico*.

So far, few anime-related games have been licensed for the U.S. market. Some fans go to the effort of making complex modifications to their game machines just so they can play the Japanese games.

I want it now: where to get the goods

More and more fans want more and more of this kind of anime-related stuff. But outside Asia it's not so easy to find the particular video, toy, picture book, or model you want. So in this section I've provided a couple shopping suggestions. While shopping, watch your wallet though, or you may find at the end of the day that you have spent everything in it.

LOCAL SHOPS

Game and toy stores often have a smattering of popular anime-related merchandise. Comics shops and hobby shops may also have some merchandise in addition to the standard videos, books, and magazines. (And, of course, if you're just looking for videos, try some of the smaller, independent rental shops; the owner may be a "fan" and have a good supply on hand.)

One advantage of local shops is that you get to look at items before buying them. (Local shops are also places where people wander in and suddenly find themselves caught in the nefarious anime net.) By developing a relationship with a retailer you can build up a reliable source of anime, manga, and related products. I encourage you to special order from your local retailers, as this tells them what you are interested in and influences their decisions about what to keep in stock.

However, even the best store can't

have everything. So at some point you must turn to other sources.

MAIL ORDER

Mail order can be a good source of merchandise, especially if your area doesn't have enough fans to support local shops ordering the products you want. (Hint: Work to increase the number of fans in your community and more anime goods will be in your local stores!)

Mail order is also useful for obtaining hard-to-get items from Japan, either directly from overseas or from an importer in your country. The disadvantage of mail order is that you can't browse and get a good look at items before buying them. Also, many exclusively mail order shops have only a limited variety of items available, mostly top sellers that they know are going to sell.

To find out about mail order sources, check the ads in anime magazines or on the Internet. Be aware that it is almost impossible for catalogs, in print or on the Internet, to list everything a store might have, so contacting mail order dealers by phone or by e-mail inquiry can often turn up that elusive object of your obsessive desire.

ANIME CONVENTIONS

Dealers' rooms at anime conventions are great places to shop for hard-to find-items, as all sorts of merchandise ends up there. Anime companies will often have tables selling their stock, including titles that have yet to ship and are elsewhere unavailable. Be prepared to use cash or checks, as not every dealer can handle credit cards. (Stock up on cash early. ATMs near the convention site empty out quickly from other fans trying to replenish their funds.) The last day of a convention is a good time to shop for bargains, so pace yourself and don't buy easy-to-find items until then. Anime conventions are pretty good about keeping pirated and bootlegged items out of the dealers' room.

INTERNET AUCTIONS

In the past few years auction sites like eBay and Amazon have become popular places to track down and buy anime merchandise. Auctions are great for folks who live in areas where there are no anime-friendly stores. But be wary of Internet auctions where the price may be inflated beyond what it would cost to buy directly. Be especially wary of people selling fansubs, which is both illegal and immoral.

Auction sites are also great places to sell stuff you already own (to raise the cash to buy more stuff perhaps?).

Pirated anime and manga goods

Anime and manga enjoy a wide popularity outside of Japan. This has resulted in some shoddy, pirated goods being available on the market. Most commonly you will find cheaply made posters and music CDs. Goods made in Japan or by U.S. companies are likely to be legitimate. The easiest way to spot a pirated poster or wall scroll is if the image is crooked or trimmed off at the edges. The Japanese have a high standard for manufactured goods, even for cheap and simple toys. So if what you are looking at is a little shoddy, be aware it may not be legit. Why avoid pirated goods? Aside from ethics, one very simple reason is that more sales of legit goods means more will be imported and available. If the market for legit merchandise grows it also means lower prices, as dealers will be able to commit to much larger orders, which in turn cuts down on the cost of shipping. All of this means cheaper and more varied goods for fans.

LIBRARIES

Consider borrowing items from your local library. Many libraries are starting to stock anime and manga. If you are a member of an anime club, have the club get together with the library staff to help them decide which anime are worth stocking. Your club could possibly even do showings in the library, which is a great way of expanding its membership. If there is no club in your area, at least talk to your librarians and see what you can do to help them get educated about anime and obtain materials for their collection. Getting anime and manga into libraries makes them more accessible to fans and non-fans alike. And if someone has already developed your local library's collection, you can enjoy the fruits of their labor and borrow all the anime you want for free!

GOING TO JAPAN AND ASIA

If you have the time and money, you may find that a trip to Japan and Asia pays off in more ways than one. You will be able to find a huge variety of items, many of them at prices far below what you would pay at home. You may also be able to find products that are simply not sold at home, due to licensing restrictions, lack of demand, or other complications. Wander down just about any street in Japan and you're bound to find a store selling wind-ups, pencils, lunchboxes, and so on, all featuring your favorite characters. I wouldn't recommend buying videos in Japan, unless you are willing to watch titles in raw Japanese (and remember that DVDs bought in Japan may not work on the system you have at home).

Japan is still a very expensive country, however, so even "cheap" Japanese toys aren't all that cheap. You may find Korea, Hong Kong, Taiwan, or even mainland China less expensive sources of supply, although, again, you run into language problems—and the potential for unknowingly buying pirated merchandise. Shops in Japan that sell used books are good places to obtain cheap manga and anime-related publications.

Don't forget—you may owe customs duty on goods you bring back from your trip overseas. Keep all your receipts. Also be aware that if you buy a lot and have to ship it home you can expect a long wait for your items to arrive. Shipping costs are a major reason imported goods cost so much, so try to send things the cheapest (which is usually the slowest) way. And while I don't encourage speculation, I do know of some people who have financed their Asian shopping adventures by loading up on anime merchandise at Asian prices and then

reselling it at home. Should you engage in such a business, remember to keep your prices fair and your product descriptions truthful! Some retailers I know make several trips a year to Japan to buy goods for their stores.

A few shopping tips

1. Be careful of impulse buying. Prices can vary between stores or even in the same store depending on what the exchange rate for the yen was when an item was imported.
2. Know your local shops. Browsing locally can be an easy way to discover new stuff.
3. Talk to the local store staff. Discuss your tastes with them and give them suggestions about forthcoming items they may not have heard about. Buy some of these items from the store to persuade them to get more.
4. Talk with other fans. They can help you locate new shops in your area or online or tell you which stores to avoid because they're selling pirated stuff. Group shopping trips are always fun, as you can ask others about items you are unsure about. It helps to share transportation if you have to travel far and long.
5. Start looking for a bigger place to live; you're going to need it.

For further guidance, check the resources I've provided in chapter 10.

NINE

41 RECOMMENDED TITLES

If you are new to anime, here's a list of 41 anime films to check out. Most of the titles here are mentioned in the body of this book; some are not. Don't see a favorite title? Well, life is like that. Had I created a longer list it probably would need a book of its own; in fact, I had to cut many titles to keep this list as short as it is. Plus, this list only includes titles available from U.S. companies; given the many new titles coming out every month, it'll probably be out of date before too long anyway (so check my web site for updates!). That said, I've taken pains to make sure this list includes titles that everyone who calls themselves a fan should be able to say they have seen (even if only in part for the longer TV series).

As you examine the credits of these and other anime, you will see the same names cropping up again and again, such as company names like Gainax, Studio Ghibli, or Bandai and its anime subsidiary, Sunrise, or the names of directors such as Studio Ghibli's Hayao Miyazaki (*My Neighbor Totoro, Kiki's Delivery Service, Princess Mononoke,* and many other films) and Isao Takahata (*Grave of the Fireflies, Only Yesterday, My Neighbors the Yamadas*); Gainax's Hideaki Anno (*Nadia: The Secret of Blue Water, GunBuster, Neon Genesis Evangelion*) and Hiroyuki Yamaga (president of Gainax and director of *The Wings of Honneamise*); or Mamoru Oshii (*Ghost in the Shell, Patlabor,* and much of *Urusei Yatsura*).

Names of musical composers you will often see include Yoko Kanno (*Macross Plus, Cowboy Bebop*) and Joe Hisaishi (*My Neighbor Totoro, Kiki's Delivery Service, Princess Mononoke,* and many other titles).

You'll frequently see the names of famous manga writers and artists whose works have been animated, like

Osamu Tezuka (*Astro Boy*, *Kimba the White Lion*, *Black Jack*) and Rumiko Takahashi (*Urusei Yatsura*, *Maison Ikkoku*, *Ranma 1/2*).

Even character designers are well known, like Kenichi Sonoda (*Gall Force*, *Gunsmith Cats*, and the original *Bubblegum Crisis* OVAs).

There are many, many more names that could be here—voice actors, producers, distribution companies, book publishers, and so on. The more anime you watch, the more these names will become familiar to you.

● ●
Tip

Rent a few tapes from a series before buying, then see if there is a box set or DVD available. Such sets are often cheaper than the same tapes sold individually. And DVDs are often cheaper than VHS as there are often more episodes on a disc than on a tape.

For parents, teachers, and librarians using this list to select (or screen) titles, I have included some notes on Japanese cultural references that may show up in the films. (See also my book *The Anime Companion: What's Japanese in Japanese Animation?*) Some parents may find occasional nudity and violence objectionable. I urge them not to stop the tape but to seri-

ously look at the story. To anyone buying anime for younger viewers, I recommend that you have respect for the intelligence of youth and not be overprotective just because of a little nudity or a little violence.

To serve only as a guide, I have where appropriate included advisories in the form of "cautions" to point out items that some parents may have reservations about. In these advisories I have defined violence broadly; in many cases it is milder than what one would see on late evening TV or on a cable movie channel. Small children may have trouble with some of these shows, while teens would not, but parents have to make their own decisions. In any case, parents with young children may want to preview tapes before sharing them with their kids, especially OVAs, which tend to be less inhibited than TV shows or movies.

Almost all of the titles listed here are available subtitled, and most are available redubbed. Many titles are on DVD. The structure for each entry in this list is title, year, original format, U.S. rightsholder. (Apologies to readers outside the U. S.!)

The box covers shown here are representative, and actual covers may differ depending on the edition.

Akira

1988, movie, Pioneer Entertainment (U.S.A.)
A well-animated story of young delinquents who accidentally get involved with a classified military experiment. The experiment may have destroyed Tokyo many years before and could again threaten it with destruction. Presently this title is unavailable. Pioneer is working on a new release. The manga was translated into English in the early 1990s and will be reissued in graphic novel form by Dark Horse. CAUTION Violence in the form of fights. Slight nudity in one scene where a girl is attacked.

Blue Seed

1995, TV series, A. D. Vision
Since she was a small child Momiji has been exposed to a series of ritual purifications and training by her grandmother. Other than that, she is a typical fourteen year old. She seems a little clumsy, struggles in school, and is just a fun kid. But one day she is threatened by a young man who mentions a twin sister she never knew she had. Then her school is attacked by something very nasty and very old that wants her dead. . . . and so the show begins. CULTURAL DETAILS Many historical sites, folklore, religion, relationships. CAUTION Fights with monsters, some character deaths. Panty humor at Momiji's expense.

BubbleGum Crisis

1987–91, OVA, AnimEigo
The OVA series of this title has been popular with English-speaking fans for many years. *BubbleGum Crisis* is a series of stories about the Knight Sabers, a mercenary group often seen fighting against an unscrupulous multinational corporation and its partially biological Boomers, a type of artificial human made for dangerous work, including use as a military weapon. An excellent example of how an OVA series can get better with each episode. Adam Warren's pseudo-manga based on this series is entitled *Bubblegum Crisis: Grand Mal* and is available in paperback from Dark Horse Comics. CAUTION Fights, some character deaths. Mild nudity in one scene.

BubbleGum Crisis 2040

1998, TV series, A. D. Vision

A different version of the story of the Knight Sabers with dramatically different character designs and a very different feel to the story. Many non-Japanese fans of the OVA were apprehensive before the series was released but liked the show when they saw it. CAUTION Fights, some character deaths.

Castle of Cagliostro

1980, movie, Manga Entertainment

One of the most popular of several Lupin III anime. After Lupin, a famous thief, and Jigen, a former hit man, find out that the cash they have stolen from a casino is phony, they end up in a small European country ruled by a count whose ways seem less pleasant than those of other nobility. Normally he would just continue on his way, but Lupin cannot ignore a fair maiden in distress, in this case the young Clarisse, unwilling fiancée to the count.

Cowboy Bebop

1998, TV series, Bandai Entertainment

Bounty hunters in the vicinity of Mars in a future gone a little seedy—but then bounty hunters seldom frequent the best part of town. Features excellent jazz music by Yoko Kanno and fine choreography for the fight scenes. The first episode was not aired on regular broadcast TV due to its storyline about drug dealers, a touchy subject in Japan. It was later broadcast in Japan on satellite TV. CAUTION Fights, some character deaths; blood is shown. Nudity in one scene; cleavage in several scenes.

El Hazard

1995, OVA, Pioneer Entertainment (U.S.A.)

Partially inspired by the pulp science fiction of Edmund Hamilton and the old *Prisoner of Zenda* movie, and with references to the science fiction works of Edgar Rice Burroughs, *El Hazard* is the tale of a young man who finds himself, along with a teacher and some schoolmates, transported to another world. A world where, it turns out, he looks very much like a missing princess. (The original OVA series is recommended over the later TV series and OVA). **CAUTION** Slapstick violence, very mild nudity, lesbian characters.

Fushigi Yūgi

1995–96, TV series, Pioneer Entertainment (U.S.A.)

A very popular shōjo anime, also known under the dub title *Mysterious Play*. Miaka likes to eat and is struggling with entrance exams so that she can get into an exclusive high school. An incident at the library transports her to another world, one very much like ancient China. She is recognized as the priestess of Shuzaku, and to get home she must gather together seven heroes. This proves to be a daunting task with strong emotional consequences. One of the heroes is gay and very sympathetically portrayed. The *Fushigi Yūgi* manga is published in the U.S. by Viz Comics. **CAUTION** Fights, some blood, character deaths, mild nudity.

Ghost in the Shell

1995, movie, Manga Entertainment

This critically acclaimed adaptation of Masamune Shirow's manga of the same title is a visually stunning science fiction tale of political intrigue. The manga is available from Dark Horse Comics in a translation by Frederik L. Schodt. **CAUTION** Violence, including a very quick and graphic death of one character; nudity.

Grave of the Fireflies

1988, movie, Central Park Media

Based on an autobiographical novel by Akiyuki Nosaka, *Grave of The Fireflies* was animated by the internationally acclaimed Studio Ghibli and directed by Isao Takahata. This beautiful tale is the tragic story of two young orphans near the end of World War II. Not an emotionally easy title to watch but widely acclaimed as a great piece of work. **CAUTION** Death of civilians in wartime.

GunBuster

1988–89, OVA, Manga Entertainment

An OVA series by Gainax, *GunBuster* is the story of Noriko, who, following her late father's footsteps, has become a space pilot. But unlike the days when her father was in space, there is now a war and the survival of all humanity is at stake. Noriko has to struggle to develop the skills she needs and to meet demands far beyond what she ever expected to come up against. CULTURAL DETAILS Locations, school life, festivals, relationships, foods. CAUTION Wartime combat, nudity in a bath scene.

The Hakkenden

1990–95, OVA, Pioneer Entertainment (U.S.A.)

An adaptation of the 19th-century novel *Nansō Satomi Hakkenden*, dense with Buddhist and Confucian symbolism, this is the tale of eight men who are somehow connected to eight virtues through separate prayer beads each one has had with him since childhood. A tale of vengeance and karma, excellent for fans of Japanese cinema and folklore.

CULTURAL DETAILS Traditional settings, clothing, locations, religious and philosophical views. CAUTION Sword fights, deaths. Too sophisticated for children, who would be bored during most of the series.

Here Is Greenwood

1991–93, OVA, Software Sculptors

Tales of Kazuya's life in a boys' high school dorm, based on a girls' manga. Both funny and serious. CULTURAL DETAILS School life, relationships, temples.

Iria: Zeiram the Animation

1994, OVA, U.S. Manga Corps

An animated version of the *Zeiram* movie, *Iria* is the science fiction story of a young bounty hunter who gets deeply involved in a case that may have resulted in the death of her brother. CAUTION Fights, character deaths.

Kiki's Delivery Service

1989, movie, Buena Vista

Kiki is a young witch, and according to tradition she must leave home at the age of thirteen, find a town with no witch, and become independent. She doesn't have many skills but her cat Jiji at least can help by offering advice. This coming-of-age tale marries a fictional European-style setting with some very stunning animation. It is another quality work directed by Hayao Miyazaki from Studio Ghibli. When it was released on video in the U. S. by Buena Vista Home Entertainment it received glowing reviews from many critics, including Roger Ebert, a longtime fan of Miyazaki's work.

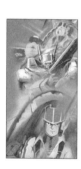

Macross

1982, TV series, AnimEigo

A landmark work. *Macross*'s combination of a popular and lengthy serialized story with mecha action and lots of music influenced much of the anime that came after it. This is the tale of a young stunt pilot who, along with many other civilians, ends up on the spaceship *Macross* when an alien attack takes place shortly before the ship's maiden voyage. A malfunctioning warp drive puts them on the edge of the Solar System, from which they must return to Earth over a period of several months. CAUTION Wartime violence, character deaths.

Macross Plus

1994–95, OVA, Manga Entertainment

Taking place long after the events of the original *Macross* TV series, this is the story of two young test pilots and a young woman who is the manager of the hottest music act in the inhabited galaxy. There is trouble in their past, and it comes back to haunt them when they find themselves reunited after they have not seen each other for seven years. (I recommend the four-tape OVA series over the movie, which is just a highly edited version of the OVA tapes with a few minutes of new animation.) Music fans will enjoy the diverse soundtrack as well as the depiction of a stadium-sized concert in the future. Residents of the San Francisco Bay Area will recognize many landmarks set on another world. CAU-TION Violence in the form of fights.

Maison Ikkoku

1986–88, TV series, Viz Video

Maison Ikkoku is the story of Godai, a young man who falls in love and has to figure out how to pursue the woman he wants. Godai is surrounded by a variety of characters—in more than one sense of the word—and must deal with his own fears and emotional clumsiness, all of which make for an entertaining series. The manga has been published in the U.S. by Viz Comics. CULTURAL DE-TAILS Foods, etiquette, household items, schools, daily life.

Martian Successor Nadesico

1996, TV series, A. D. Vision

A multilayered story told through rich animation. A comedy? A drama? A science fiction program? A giant robot show? A spoof of anime fans? A love story? Yes! And very popular with fans. The manga is published in the U.S. by CPM Manga.

Mobile Suit Gundam

The *Mobile Suit Gundam* series of anime shows has been a major part of anime since 1979, when the first series was broadcast on TV. The quality of the shows varies, but many are excellent, highly dramatic works worthy of consideration as being among the best in anime.

The original story is set in the future when most of humanity has relocated into clusters of artificial space colonies called "sides." Each side is composed of several colonies; the older, smaller colonies hold about 3 million inhabitants, the larger ones about 15 million.

A new calendar is in use, dating from the settlement of the first colonies. Many of the shows are titled according to the year in which they take place. In 0079, one side revolts against Earth rule, establishes the Zeon dictatorship, and attacks the Earth Federation with little warning.

In the first year of war half of humanity is wiped out: 5 billion dead. A result of this is the Treaty of Antarctica banning nuclear weapons, poison gas, and the destruction of colonies. A major type of weapon has come into existence: large and usually anthropomorphic Mobile Suits designed for close combat. Long-distance combat has been rendered useless by the discovery of Minovsky particles that, when scattered, block radio and radar and effectively eliminate many of the techniques of modern warfare.

A major theme in the *Gundam* series is the effect of warfare on civilian populations. While the shows take place in wartime, they are not simple action entertainment. Several of the manga are being published by Viz Comics and Mixx Entertainment. CAUTION Combat; all *Gundam* shows take place during wartime.

Mobile Suit Gundam: The Movies

1981, movie, Bandai Entertainment
The series was formed by taking the TV shows and reediting them into three movies. The movies provide the background for the rest of the *Gundam* shows. The story is of a group of civilian refugees who are drafted to help run a ship carrying themselves, other refugees, and a new kind of experimental mobile suit known as Gundam.

Mobile Suit Gundam 0080

1989, OVA, Bandai Entertainment
The dramatic story of Al, a young boy living on a neutral colony who struggles to cope with the separation of his parents and with trouble in school. One day he ends up befriending a young Zeon soldier who is actually part of a group investigating a hidden Federation research facility.

Mobile Suit Gundam 0083

1991–92, OVA, Bandai Entertainment
The war is over but some elements of the old Zeon troops feel that they cannot live with the peace treaty. They attempt to start a new war by stealing and using a special experimental Gundam unit armed with a nuclear warhead. Among the crew of the Federation ship sent to recover the stolen Gundam is Nina Purpleton, a young woman engineer who is in charge of the stolen experimental Gundam unit as well as of another experimental Gundam unit that was not stolen. ›

My Neighbor Totoro

1988, movie, Fox Video

Hayao Miyazaki's tale of two young girls who move to a country house with their father during what appears to be the 1950s. The mother is ill, and the world is alive with magical furry creatures, including one the girls call Totoro. This title is very popular with parents and children. Helen McCarthy notes that Akira Kurosawa was so impressed with Miyazaki's work that he included *My Neighbor Totoro* in his list of the hundred best films ever made, a distinction shared by few Japanese directors. (Released in the United States by Fox, the license for this title will expire soon and the distribution rights transfer to Disney.) CULTURAL DETAILS Household details, country life. CAUTION Mild nudity during a scene when the father takes a bath with his two daughters, a normal parent/child bonding activity in Japan.

Nadia: The Secret of Blue Water

1990–91, TV series,
A. D. Vision

The story is loosely based on Jules Verne's great science fiction novel *20,000 Leagues Under the Sea*. Perhaps "inspired by" would be a better term. *Nadia: The Secret of Blue Water* is a rich and well-crafted work about a young inventor, Jean, who meets a young, dark-skinned circus performer, Nadia. Jean helps Nadia escape from a woman and two thugs who are trying to get her and the gem she wears around her neck. After their dramatic getaway, Jean and Nadia set out to find about Nadia's past, and so the adventure begins. The two are then pursued by more than one group after the gem. . . . but I'm getting ahead of the events in the first tape. This series was made for NHK, the Japanese national broadcasting system. CAUTION Occasional violence, slapstick, some character deaths.

Neon Genesis Evangelion

1995–96, TV series, A. D. Vision

This highly acclaimed TV series from the Gainax studio was aimed at an older audience. It is a science fiction extravaganza more about human feelings and trust than about dealing with some very alien attackers. The manga is available in the U.S. from Viz Comics. **CULTURAL DETAILS** Foods, etiquette, locations. **CAUTION** Violence, character deaths, some mild sexual humor.

Oh My Goddess!

1993, OVA, AnimEigo

A heartwarming and humorous story of a young man granted a wish by a visiting goddess. Thinking it a joke, he makes a decision (which I won't reveal) with some very unexpected results. As the story develops, the bond between him and the goddess Belldandy grows deeper. The manga is available in the U.S. from Dark Horse Comics. **CULTURAL DETAILS** Foods, locations, architecture, household items, college life. **CAUTION** Mild comedic sexual situation in one episode.

Patlabor

This series is both a personal favorite and one that all fans should see. Due to several *Patlabor* titles existing in different formats—OVAs, a TV series and movies—this section is a bit long.

In the near future, advances in mechanical and computer technology have resulted in the development of new construction machines called Labors. As Labors become more widely used for legitimate purposes, there is also a rise in their employment in crime. The *Patlabor* series is about a special police unit in Tokyo charged with dealing with Labor crime. (Patlabor is a short way of saying Patrol Labor.) The series revolves around the people involved in the Patlabor unit, especially a young policewoman named Noa Izumi. As the series develops, so does our knowledge of the characters. *Patlabor* is also known as *Patlabor the Mobile Police* and *Mobile Police Patlabor.* A manga series is partially available in paperback from Viz Comics. **CULTURAL DETAILS** Tokyo locations, etiquette, expressions of feelings, foods.

Patlabor: The Mobile Police—The Original Series

1988–89, OVA, U.S. Manga Corps.
The original series of stories that introduces us to the characters and their lives.

Patlabor TV Series

1990–91, TV series, U.S. Manga Corps.
Reintroduces the characters in a different way, as there is no way to be sure that the TV show viewers had seen the original OVAs. TV shows based on OVAs often reintroduce chara, changing the storyline slightly as they do.

Patlabor: The New Files

1990–92, OVA, U.S. Manga Corps.
A series of stories, some of which continue plots from the TV series.

Patlabor 1

1989, movie, Manga Entertainment
Labors require very complex software, so complex that the machines have to be "trained" to work with a particular operator. What happens when a major upgrade to the operating system contains a virus, and how can the potential destruction be avoided? Directed by Mamoru Oshii.

Patlabor 2

1993, movie, Manga Entertainment
Something mysterious is going on. The threat of a military coup involving factions of the Japanese military with American backing brings the country to the brink of disaster. And someone in the Patrol Labor units has a personal history with a major player. Directed by Mamoru Oshii.

Perfect Blue

1998, movie, Manga Entertainment

A very complex and highly cinematic anime about Mima, a young woman who has abandoned her stalled career as an idol singer to become an actress. Mima gets a major supporting role in a TV mystery series and is willing to do things in front of the camera to further her acting career that her former fans dislike. Someone objects to the destruction of the innocent image Mima had as a singer; this "objection" becomes very dangerous. Not for lightweights, this anime has a complex plot that is tied up nicely at the end. In 1997, before it was even shown in theaters in Japan, *Perfect Blue* won Best Asian Film at the Fant-Asia Movie Festival in Montreal. This is the first work directed by Satoshi Kon, an artist whose previous anime work had consisted of doing storyboards for a segment of the *Memories* anime. CAUTION Violence, nudity. Not at all for kids.

Princess Mononoke

1997, movie, Buena Vista

This movie became the all-time highest grossing Japanese movie in a matter of a few weeks. It is the story of a young man who becomes cursed in the form of a strange wound after killing an enraged giant boar *kami* (god). He leaves his village to seek out the source of the boar god's anger, hoping that this will result in a cure. What he discovers is a conflict between the *kami* of a forest and some settlers who have set up an iron mining and smelting operation. But unlike heroes in American cinema, he does not take sides in the battle, even when things get very dangerous. Directed by Hayao Miyazaki (*Kiki's Delivery Service, My Neighbor Totoro*). CAUTION Warfare, deaths, blood.

Ranma 1/2

1989–92, TV series, Viz Video

The third anime adaptation of a Rumiko Takahashi manga. Ranma is a young martial artist under an unfortunate curse. Akane is Ranma's fiancée through an arrangement between their fathers. Much of the story is about how these two strong-willed children deal with the situation they find themselves in. I recommend concentrating on the TV series, as the movies and OVAs have characters that enter the TV series quite late in the game. An unfortunate example of misleading wording is how the early tape boxes describe the series as a "sex comedy." A better choice of words would have been "gender comedy," since the story pokes fun at traditional male/female roles and there is no sexual activity depicted. The manga is available in the U.S. from Viz Comics. CULTURAL DETAILS School life, martial arts, relationships, foods, clothing, traditional home and garden. CAUTION Slapstick martial arts combat, mild nudity.

Revolutionary Girl Utena

1997–98, TV series
Software Sculptors
One of the most shōjo of all anime available in the U.S. It is the story of Utena, a tomboyish student in a very unusual school. After the death of her parents, Utena as a small child was comforted by a prince, and this inspired her to grow up and become a prince herself. The prince gave her the ring she wears, a ring that identifies her as a member of a select group who duel for control of the Rose Bride. (What, or who, is the Rose Bride? Watch episode one and find out.) Soon Utena finds herself caught up in the duels and in a strange series of events somehow linked to the prince from her childhood. CAUTION Sword duels, nonexplicit sexual situations. Not for little kids, who might ask embarrassing questions.

Serial Experiments Lain

1998, TV series, Pioneer Entertainment (U.S.A.)
An award-winning TV series about human interaction with technology. Lain is a young girl whose interest in computers is sparked when she receives e-mail from a girl in her school. Except the e-mail was sent after the girl had jumped from a tall building to her death. . . . CULTURAL DETAILS School life, relationships, foods. CAUTION Deaths, blood.

Tenchi Muyo

1992–95, OVA, Pioneer Entertainment (U.S.A.)
I recommend the original OVA series over the much lighter TV series. One day, Tenchi sneaks into a cave on the grounds of the family shrine and ends up releasing a demon who has been imprisoned there for centuries. Tenchi believes he has succeeded in resealing the demon in the cave until it visits him one night looking for revenge; it turns out that it was one of Tenchi's ancestor's who had confined the demon there in the first place. Even if you don't watch the TV series, the *Tenchi* OVAs, which follow the TV series plot lines, are worth seeing as the characters are the same. The manga is available in the U.S. from Viz Comics. CAUTION Some characters end up fighting to save others.

Urusei Yatsura

1981–86, all formats, AnimEigo
This is a big franchise. Eventually there will be something like fifty TV tapes or DVD discs (100 minutes each), six OVA tapes, and six movie tapes. *Urusei Yatsura* is a very popular series with fans and is the first anime series based on the works of Rumiko Takahashi. Ataru is far more than your typical high school sex fiend. When we first see him he is drooling after watching a beautiful woman walk by. But the Earth is about to be invaded, and the aliens' computer has chosen Ataru to be Earth's champion in a competition. To win, he has to grab the horns of the alien princess Lum, who happens to have a great figure and wear a bikini. But no one told Ataru that Lum could fly! To encourage him, Ataru's girlfriend offers to marry him if he succeeds. So when Ataru finally grabs Lum's horns he announces that he can finally get married. Lum, thinking he means her, accepts. And so the story begins. The manga is available in the U.S. from Viz Comics. CULTURAL DETAILS Day to day life, school, foods, locations, folklore, gender relations. CAUTION Despite the summary above, there's nothing more harmful here than lots of silly stuff . . . and some merciless satire.

Vampire Princess Miyu

1988–89, OVA, AnimEigo

A series of interconnected stories about a woman trying to track down a young female vampire. The vampire for some reason is killing and banishing demons. The tale overall is somewhat moody and dramatic. The manga is available in the U.S. from Studio Ironcat. CULTURAL DETAILS Historical locations, architecture, school life. CAUTION Could be frightening for small children.

The Wings of Honneamise

1987, movie, Manga Entertainment

The Wings of Honneamise was the first production by a group of animators who at the time were largely unknown in the industry. It surprised critics and fans with its sophistication and raised the standards for the entire industry. Gainax, the studio that produced this title, has gone on to be one of the most innovative and successful animation companies in Japan; other Gainax films include GunBuster and *Neon Genesis Evangelion*. Directed by Hiroyuki Yamaga. CAUTION Violence in a couple of scenes.

You're Under Arrest

1994–95, OVA, AnimEigo

A fun series of tales about traffic police in modern Tokyo. The original four OVAs were followed by a TV series in Japan and an animated movie. The TV series begins with episode 5, following the four OVAs, an unusual numbering system. The manga is available in the U.S. from Dark Horse Comics. CULTURAL DETAILS Locations, foods, daily life.

TEN

ANIME RESOURCES

Here are some good places to find out more about Japanese animation.

Books

This section only lists books devoted entirely to anime and manga. Books with single chapters and essays on these subjects are not included, nor are various academic works, including dissertations and journal articles, of interest.

The ISBN number that appears with each listing is the unique identifier for each edition of every book published, and can be used for ordering at stores or online. In most cases, however, the author and title should suffice.

Allison, Anne. *Permitted and Prohibited Desires: Mothers, Comics and Censorship in Japan.* Hardcover. Boulder: Westview Press, 1996.

ISBN 0-8133-1698-7. (Paperback. Berkeley: University of California Press; ISBN 0-520-21990-2.)

An anthropological study of gender in erotic manga in Japan. Professor Allison based this book on five years of research in a middle-class neighborhood in Tokyo. Using theories from feminist anthropology and Marxism, this work covers a broad range of aspects of the content of erotic manga.

Baricordi, Andrea; Massimiliano De Giovanni; Andrea Pietroni; Barbara Rossi; and Sabrina Tunesi. *Anime: A Guide to Japanese Animation (1958–1988).* Translated by Adeline D'Opera. Montreal: Protoculture, 2000. ISBN 2-9805759-0-9.

A guide to anime produced in this period. Originally published in Italy.

Kinsella, Sharon. *Adult Manga: Culture and Power in Contemporary Japanese Society*. Honolulu: University of Hawaii Press, 2000. ISBN 0-8248-2318-4.

A study of the development and transformation of the adult manga industry in Japan. Includes information on the dōjinshi subculture and connections between the movements for manga censorship and political parties or government agencies. First published in the United Kingdom by Curzon Press.

Ledoux, Trish, and Doug Ranney. *The Complete Anime Guide*. 2nd edition. Issaquah, Washington: Tiger Mountain Press, 1997. ISBN 0-9649542-5-7.

This work begins with a few short essays on anime and is mostly a catalog of anime released in the U.S. up to the date of the book's publication. It includes a history of anime shown on U.S. TV from 1963 to 1996, a look at anime genres, and information on fan groups. While out of date, the catalog section is still a useful reference tool for shoppers.

Ledoux, Trish, ed. *Anime Interviews: The First Five Years of* Animerica Anime *and* Manga Monthly *(1992–97)*. San Francisco: Cadence Books, 1997. ISBN 1-56931-220-6.

I am one of those people who always says that the best part of *Animerica* magazine is the interviews. Each interview reproduced in this book is accompanied by a bibliography/filmography related to the person interviewed.

Levi, Antonia. *Samurai From Outer Space: Understanding Japanese Animation*. Chicago: Open Court, 1996. ISBN 0-8126-9332-9.

Antonia Levi is both an anime fan and a professor of Japanese history. In this popular book, Dr. Levi places much of what you see in anime in its cultural context.

McCarthy, Helen. *Anime! A Beginner's Guide to Japanese Animation*. London: Titan Books, 1993. ISBN 1-85286-492-3.

The first English-language book on anime and the spiritual ancestor of this book. When McCarthy's book came out in 1993, much of what is listed in it was not available in English. In fact many titles have yet to be released in either subtitled or redubbed versions. Anime fandom then was much smaller than it is now and was largely centered on individuals active in science fiction fandom or college clubs. The book is now out of print but is occasionally seen in secondhand book shops.

 McCarthy, Helen. *The Anime Movie Guide*. London: Titan Books, 1996. ISBN 1-85286-631-4. (New York: Overlook Press, 1997. ISBN 0-87951-781-6.)

A guide to anime movies and OVAs released between 1983 and the end of 1995. Not covered are TV series rereleased on video. This book contains excellent short articles on many aspects of anime along with descriptions of the anime covered, including many anime not yet released in English.

 McCarthy, Helen, and Jonathan Clements. *The Erotic Anime Movie Guide*. London: Titan Books, 1998. ISBN 1-85286-946-1. (New York: Overlook Press, 1999. ISBN 0879517050.)

An excellent study of eroticism in anime. The authors felt there was a need to look at one of the more controversial aspects of anime and have produced a balanced and interesting work. Because the filmography section is so small and has so many films that are not explicitly sexual, we can see that that this branch of anime is really not very large.

 McCarthy, Helen. *Hayao Miyazaki: Master of Japanese Animation*. Berkeley: Stone Bridge Press, 1999. ISBN 1-880656-41-8.

This book starts with a general survey of Miyazaki's life and work and then covers his anime titles one by one. The coverage of the anime is especially nice; for each title it includes the origins, the techniques used, the characters, a summary of the story, and a commentary. I was especially glad to see the completeness of the filmography, which covers the major works plus other titles Miyazaki had a relatively minor part in. This book belongs on the shelves not only of every anime fan but of every fan of Japanese cinema.

Omega, Ryan. *The Anime Trivia Quizbook: Episode One, From Easy to Otaku Obscure*. Berkeley: Stone Bridge Press, 2000. ISBN 1-880656-44-2.

I'm not a trivia game fan, so when I first opened this book I did not really know how to judge it. But it quickly became apparent that this is not just a trivia book about anime but an entertaining dialogue between author and reader. The book is broken down into broad categories such as Mascots, Merchandise, Cultural, Video Games, and many others. Each page of questions has the answers on the back of the same page, making it very easy to use this book for instant trivia contests with your friends.

Poitras, Gilles. *The Anime Companion: What's Japanese in Japanese Animation?* Berkeley: Stone Bridge Press, 1998. ISBN 1-880656-32-9.

My own book focusing on anime as a window from which to view and to learn about Japanese culture. Most of the book is a dictionary of "objects" seen in anime. These include furniture, historical personages, organizations, corporations, etiquette, gestures, foods, and any other detail I could locate information on.

Princess Mononoke: The Art and Making of Japan's Most Popular Film of All Time. New York: Hyperion, 1999. ISBN 0-7868-6609-8.

An English-language translation, with introduction by Mark Schilling, of the Japanese book *The Art of Princess Mononoke*. For any fan of the works of Miyazaki, this is a rich collection of images from and information about the *Mononoke Hime* anime.

Schodt, Frederik L. *Dreamland Japan: Writings on Modern Manga*. Berkeley: Stone Bridge Press, 1996. ISBN 1-880656-23-X.

A collection of essays on the manga phenomenon in Japan, with chapters on the history of manga, its common genres, the artists and writers, and some of the magazines devoted to manga. A must for any fan trying to understand the genres in anime.

Schodt, Frederik L. *Manga! Manga! The World of Japanese Comics*. Tokyo, New York, and London: Kodansha International, 1983. ISBN 0-87011-752-1.

The first, and still very useful, English-language book about manga. Includes a section of translations from four different works. Highly recommended for a general overview of this significant branch of Japanese publishing. Like the author's *Dreamland Japan*, an important book for anime fans.

Magazines

ENGLISH-LANGUAGE MAGAZINES

Animeco
Limelight Publishing
4224 Waialae Avenue, #339
Honolulu, HI 96816
http://www.ishopper.com/limelight/animeco.html

While published irregularly, *Animeco* is a fun magazine with a strong fan focus. Articles cover a wide range of topics related to anime and Japanese popular culture. Each issue includes a large selection of short reviews. The publisher keeps back issues in stock, so it is easy to get a full run.

Animerica: Anime and Manga Monthly
Viz Communications
P.O. Box 77010
San Francisco, CA 94107
http://www.animerica-mag.com/

Almost every issue of *Animerica* contains an interview with a major figure in anime and articles focusing on particular anime related to the person interviewed. Short reviews of anime, manga, games, and music CDs appear in each issue. About 30 percent of each issue is devoted to a translation of a serialized manga.

Manga Max

Titan Magazines
42–44 Dolben Street
London SE1 0UP
England
Manga Max contains more than just articles on anime. It also has excellent coverage of manga and live-action Asian films. One of the strengths of *Manga Max* is its coverage of older shows, which provides information for newer fans of what came before. The magazine is easily obtainable in the U.S.

Protoculture Addicts

P.O. Box 1433
Station "B"
Montreal
Quebec H3B 3L2
Canada
http://www.protocul ture.qc.ca/PA/
Each issue of *Protoculture Addicts* spotlights one anime, often a title that has yet to be released in the U.S. The articles are in great detail, with synopses of longer TV shows occasionally spanning several issues. Also there is coverage of various books, manga, soundtracks, and general news.

JAPANESE-LANGUAGE MAGAZINES
There are lots of Japanese magazines devoted to anime, manga, and related subjects. Among the more well known and easier to obtain outside Japan are *Animage, AX,* and *New Type* for anime and *B-Magazine, Hobby Japan,* and *Model Graphix* for model builders. Some of these are distributed to comic shops by the wholesaler Diamond Comics (www.diamondcomics.com). More titles are commonly available at Japanese shops or shops that specialize in anime and related merchandise.

Internet resources

The Internet is a familiar place to anime fans. A decade or more before the public was familiar with the term, anime fans communicated over the Internet, and the smaller Fidonet, via email, FTP sites, and BBS systems.

Today the Internet is touted as the motherload of information. But try to find anything of substance quickly and you are bound to be frustrated. Searching for facts on the Internet is like searching for tape 2 of the *Oh My Goddess!* OVA series after a major earthquake has dumped everything off the shelves of your local megavideo store. You know roughly where to look but have to push through lots of irrelevant stuff first—assuming what you want was even there to begin with.

The ephemeral nature of the Web, which is what most people think of when they say Internet, is another problem. Web sites move, morph, or vanish. For this reason I am including only a few web sites here, sites that are starting places for finding information and sites that are likely to still be there in the future.

There are three major types of resources for anime fans that are available via the Internet: web-based resources, Usenet newsgroups, and lists.

THE WORLD WIDE WEB

By now the web is well known enough that I do not have to explain it here. Suffice it to say that all you need is a browser and an internet service provider and you're in business.

Anime Web Turnpike
www.anipike.com/

Founded in 1995, Anime Web Turnpike is the best and most famous topical guide to Internet resources on anime and manga. This is a good place to begin looking for information. Especially useful are its links to company web sites, pages put up by anime clubs and conventions, sites devoted to specific series, and many excellent online reference tools or databases.

EX: The Online World of Anime and Manga
www.ex.org

This is actually a web-based magazine that began publishing in June of 1996. Expect the same type of articles one would get from a good movie magazine. EX is a site all anime fans should read. You can even subscribe to a service that notifies you when new issues are released.

Nausicaa.net
www.nausicaa.net/

A fan site focusing on the works of Studio Ghibli and its directors, most notably Hayao Miyazaki. One of the most impressive series of web pages I have ever seen on any topic, it is like an online reference work for the fans of one of the best animation studios in the world.

Seiyuu: Voice Actor Database
www.tcp.com/doi/seiyuu/seiyuu.html
Just as movie fans follow the releases of favorite film actors, anime fans keep up with their favorite voice actors. This database of actors and their roles in anime and games also includes musical recordings, recorded dramas, performance videos, and magazines as well as radio and TV shows.

And finally, here are a few pages of my own that I hope are of use to fans:

Shopping Report
www.sirius.com/ ~ cowpunk/ shopping.html
Once a week I report on anime and manga that have actually been seen in stores. It is a handy place to verify the release of a title, since the scheduled release date is often not the actual one. The worst example was a video released over six months after the announced date, with no announcement from the publisher. I will not say who did this.

USA Anime and Manga Report
www.sirius.com/ ~ cowpunk/ USAAnimeRelease.html
My monthly newsletter consisting of reviews, industry news, and release dates and order information for anime and manga titles to be released in the U.S. I attempt to be comprehensive in reporting the shipping dates for every U.S. release of an anime or manga translation.

Anime Companion Supplement
www.sirius.com/ ~ cowpunk/ ACmain.html
A supplement to my earlier book *The Anime Companion*. Its purpose is to keep the material contained in the book up to date by adding new material, links to related Internet resources, and additions to material covered in the book.

USENET NEWSGROUPS
While the World Wide Web runs on top of the Internet, Usenet is not limited to the Internet and has long been available from other kinds of networks, although these networks are largely being replaced by the Internet.

Usenet provides access to a major resource on the Internet, other people. It is divided up into subject specific "newsgroups." A newsgroup is a good place to go if you are looking for information on a topic, or just wish to discuss something. The words "subject specific" are important here, as it is considered bad manners to stray away from the subject of a newsgroup. Do not discuss anime in a manga news-group or *Utena* in the *Gundam* news-group. You cannot read a newsgroup unless your internet service provider (ISP) makes it available on its news-server. If a newsgroup you want is not available through your ISP simply ask them to add it.

To read newsgroups, you can use a web browser that includes the ability to read newsgroups (not all browsers do) or a separate newsgroup-reading tool. Consult with your ISP as to which newsgroup software they recommend.

I am only listing the main English-language newsgroups here. Check the Anime Web Turnpike listings for a more complete list. Many newsgroups are in languages other than English.

• •
Tip

Lurk in, or just read, a newsgroup for a while before posting.

The newsgroup names are general-ly self-explanatory of the newsgroup content.

GENERAL NEWSGROUPS
rec.arts.anime.creative
rec.arts.anime.fandom
rec.arts.anime.games
rec.arts.anime.info

rec.arts.anime.marketplace
rec.arts.anime.misc
rec.arts.anime.models
rec.arts.anime.music
rec.arts.manga
uk.media.animation.anime (for the
  UK)

NEWSGROUPS DEVOTED TO SPECIFIC TITLES
alt.anime.gundam
alt.fan.bgcrisis
alt.fan.dragonball
alt.fan.macross
alt.fan.sailor-moon
alt.fan.utena

NEWSGROUP DEVOTED TO A SPECIFIC PERSON
alt.fan.r-takahashi

LISTS
"Lists" is the term commonly used to refer to electronic mailing lists. Such lists work on a simple principle. There is a single address for the list, and any message sent to this address is passed on to anyone who subscribes to the list. There may be only a few dozen subscribers, or there may be thou-sands. This means that if you sub-scribe to a list or two you can get more e-mail than you can easily handle. For this reason I prefer Usenet over lists for ease of use, since in Usenet you can

simply ignore discussions you are not interested in. That said, many lists are not very busy and are worth subscribing to if you really like the topic.

● ●
Tip

When you first subscribe to a list you get a confirmation message. Be sure to save that message; it contains the proper method for unsubscribing along with other useful information.

I am not including a "list of lists," as lists are quite volatile and subject to change. Lists commonly change servers, and subscription techniques vary according to the software the server uses. Instead, I suggest checking the Anime Web Turnpike for information on lists or asking in the appropriate newsgroups about lists on your favorite topics. Many lists are not mentioned on the Turnpike, perhaps to restrict access to the more serious fans by making them a little harder for folks to find.

There are web sites that provide information about lists in general. Two of the better ones are:

List of Lists
catalog.com/vivian/interest-group-search.html
One of the oldest such resources, searchable.

Liszt: The Mailing List Directory
www.liszt.com/
A searchable database of mailing lists.

SUBJECT INDEX

OTAKU NO VIDEO: THE LAST LESSON

©1991 GAINAX /YOUMEX

OK, like Kubo here you still have a lot of studying to do. Pick an area of anime interest and get reading or working. Don't focus too narrowly, but switch activities occasionally. And, as a non-Japanese, try your hand at learning the Japanese language so you can watch anime and read manga that have yet to be translated (there are plenty!). Of course, also spend some time studying Japanese culture, especially the food. . . .